TWO WOMEN DANCING

Elizabeth Bartlett (1924-2008) was born in Deal, in the mining region of Kent. She left school at 15 shortly before the start of the Second World War, to start work in a factory making hypodermic needles. Married during the War, she helped support her family with various jobs, working for 16 years as a medical secretary, and later in the home help service and as a tutor. She lived in Burgess Hill, West Sussex.

Despite early success at the age of 19, in Tambimuttu's *Poetry London*, she did not publish again until her mid-50s. Her first retrospective volume, *A Lifetime of Dying: Poems 1942-1979* (Peterloo Poets, 1979), covered mainly work written in the latter two decades. She went on to publish four collections in the 1980s and early 90s: *Strange Territory* (Peterloo Poets, 1983), *The Czar Is Dead* (Rivelin Grapheme, 1986), *Instead of a Mass* (Headland, 1991) and *Look, No Face* (Redbeck Press, 1991).

In 1995 Bloodaxe published *Two Women Dancing: New & Selected Poems*, edited by Carol Rumens, which was a Poetry Book Society Recommendation. This was followed by two later collections of poems written in her late 70s, *Appetites of Love* (2001) and *Mrs Perkins and Oedipus* (2004), both from Bloodaxe. In 2005 the Poetry Archive issued her CD, *Elizabeth Bartlett Reading from her poems*.

ELIZABETH BARTLETT

Two Women Dancing

NEW & SELECTED POEMS

EDITED BY CAROL RUMENS

BLOODAXE BOOKS

ISBN: 978 1 85224 297 8

First published 1995 by
Bloodaxe Books Ltd,
Eastburn,
South Park,
Hexham,
Northumberland NE46 1BS.

www.bloodaxebooks.com
For further information about Bloodaxe titles
please visit our website or write to
the above address for a catalogue.

Supported using public funding by

**ARTS COUNCIL
ENGLAND**

Digital reprint of the 1995 Bloodaxe Books edition.

for my son, Alexander

Acknowledgements

This selection includes work from Elizabeth Bartlett's collections *A Lifetime of Dying: Poems 1942-1979* (Peterloo Poets, 1979), *Strange Territory* (Peterloo Poets, 1983), *The Czar is Dead* (Rivelin Grapheme Press, 1986), *Instead of a Mass* (Headland, 1991) and *Look, No Face* (Redbeck Press, 1991).

For the new poems in the *Two Women Dancing* section of the book, acknowledgements are due to the editors of these publications in which some of the poems first appeared: *Ambit, Blue Buildings* (USA), *Critical Quarterly, Cumberland Review* (USA), *Forward Anthology* (Forward Publishing, 1993), *The Guardian, National Poetry Competition Anthology* (Poetry Society, 1989), *Orbis, Outposts, Oxford Poetry, Poems from the Medical World* (MTP Press, 1980), *Poetry London, Poetry Nottingham, Poetry Review, Poetry with an Edge* (Bloodaxe Books, new edition, 1993), *Prospice, Sixty Women Poets* (Bloodaxe Books, 1993), *Staple, Times Literary Supplement, Tribune, Writers at Hanover, Voices from Arts for Labour* (Pluto Press, 1985) and *Writing Women*.

The comments by Elizabeth Bartlett quoted in the Introduction are from an interview between Elizabeth Bartlett and Carol Rumens which is to be published in *Poetry Review*.

Contents

Two Women Dancing (1995)

INTRODUCTION

1

Elizabeth Bartlett's poetry has been tagged with such labels as 'feminist' and 'working-class', but might be more usefully seen in a broader context, that of the published amateur. The term 'amateur' is not intended to denigrate. Many English poets, historically, have been drawn from such a group and, despite the development this century of poetry as a profession, or professionalism, it remains large and flourishing. It is literature's heartbeat, linking it to the bloodstream of the vernacular, yet allowing an openness and iconoclasm that may finally leave post-modernism and its self-conscious dislocations in the shade.

Such poets are outside the academy and resistant to its demarcation lines and theories (a matter of particular irony in the case of women poets). They may in fact never have undergone the formative experience of tertiary education. Their supporting careers – if they have them – are as unlikely to be in the literary media as in the academy. They may publish sporadically, mostly, though not exclusively, in the small presses, and they may well be late starters, particularly if they are women.

Poets of this kind could perhaps be grouped by their resistance to groups. Elizabeth Bartlett, for example, belongs to the same generation as the English 'Movement' poets, and her work does share some of the Movement's broad concerns. But, developing later than these writers, she forges ahead of them in thematic scope and emotional honesty, and shows an entirely independent way with form and metre. She has more in common with a younger generation of writers, including poets such as Peter Reading and Carol Ann Duffy, whose work may also reflect her influence.

'I am skilled at closing eyes / and singing grace notes, / as well as changing sheets,' the narrator of 'Lyke-Wake' drily remarks. This duality of roles, reflected in the title of this book (the 'two women dancing' are most likely two aspects of one woman) is a constant theme which has given rise to a characteristic technique. Bartlett likes to work in a kind of two-part counterpoint, cutting, for example, between scenes from novels and 'real life' in 'W.E.A. Course', or interweaving private and public concerns, as in 'A Straw Mat'. Her sometimes breathtaking self-confidence in dealing with desperate situations and characters *in extremis* surely derives not only from practical experience but from her sense that the poet is not remote from human pathology, but one of its forms.

A certain amount of interrogation concerning the value of poetry and of her contribution to it, hangs in the air around Elizabeth Bartlett's work. She often ironises herself as the poet-figure, sometimes with slightly heavy-handed self-consciousness, as in 'Biographical Note', but also with wit and bravado. In 'My Five Gentlemen' she writes amusingly of being at the mercy of an all-male literary power structure: 'Prostitutes have clients, wives have husbands / Poets, you will understand, have editors.' Her hope, finally, to be 're-cycled / And end up more useful than I would appear to be', surely gives the poet the last laugh, since poems may live for readers' recyclings long after editors are forgotten. Her most characteristic poems, however, focus on a world in which poetry matters very little indeed, and derive rebellious energy from that fact.

This is the instantly recognisable world of welfare-state, working-class, post-war England ('her mad, sick, anywhere country'), taking in the suburban-genteel aspects, the Oxfam shops and rush-matted, cat-haunted middle-class interiors as well as the grimly urban or institutional settings for which she is best known. Though her imagination has an inventive, story-telling side, and enjoys creating surreal effects, the power of much of the work lies in Bartlett's willingness to reveal the situation in front of her, with just as much art as is necessary to develop and print the film. From casual-seeming lists of detail she can build a set which has both specific and symbolic presence ('Polling Station', 'Lisson Grove', etc). Her characters are allowed to be individuals, perhaps by the device of being named (Ian, David, Kim, Maggie, et al), or by having brief but extremely effective speaking-parts, recorded with a novelist's ear for the vernacular.

There is undoubtedly a powerful social conscience underlying her work, and she trains its focus on a wide range of concerns: green politics, for example, are a recent preoccupation. But social criticism is not the goal. Bartlett writes effectively about issues because she does not detach them from inner pressures. The cracks in the public building also fissure the individual's subconscious, and vice versa.

Of her writing about suffering and oppression, she says: 'For me, it was what was close to hand to write about, part of daily life observed,' going on to quote T.S. Eliot's view of poetry as 'only the relief of a personal and wholly insignificant grouse against life; it is just a piece of rhythmical grumbling'.

If the phrase 'rhythmical grumbling' hardly does justice to the angry intensity achieved in a poem like 'Corpus Christi', it remains suggestive in highlighting the authentic and personal elements in her response. The diction here is appropriately low-key, sometimes even off-hand. Bland institutional pieties are mimed in euphemisms like 'children in care' or the ironical shorthand of 'kindly over-worked staff', but the driving rhythm pushes such language beyond its own banality. One of the interesting small by-products of contemporary poetry is the reclamation of the cliché. Elizabeth Bartlett's work does the equivalent for 'admin-speak', not by honing the words to outlines of lost precision but by pitching them along in a rhythmically charged narrative that can achieve the intensity of a tragic vision. As the 'tarted-up Adult Education Centre' of 'Corpus Christi' is haunted by its past as 'a receiving place for children in care', so a language bare of metaphor and almost prosaic is undercut by darker, older English sonorities and spellings:

> Corpus Christi I think I shall choose for next week's chilly session,
> Feeling a wounde that is always bledyng as they lie upon their beds,
> With comics under their pillows and nits in their little heds.
> Their hearts are surely turned to ston, Corpus Christi wretyn thereon.

A dialogue with tradition is going on in much of Bartlett's work. The poems often enact interesting negotiations between the formal "big stanza" with its regular metre and rhyme, and vernacular looseness. Her line-formation never breaks faith with the rhythms of modern English speech. Yet the metrical 'ghost' is a vital presence and reference. It not only satisfies the reader's often-neglected need for melody, but allows the work to subvert, play with and ironically comment on English traditions and at the same time draw strength from them. Generations of love-poems and elegies underwrite some of her grittiest settings. Her treatment of the love poem ranges from 'Design', an early work (1942) that is both imagistic and pastoral, its light-filled landscape shot through with intimations of 'et in Arcadia ego' that suggest an early mentor, Edward Thomas, to 'Waiting Room' with its hospital setting and sense of mortal love made grimly flesh among the 'daily trivia' of 'forms for x-rays', 'scrips for killing pain' and 'all those crazy get-well tokens which/ clutter up lockers as if a birthday had come'. In many poems, the tone, far from being 'grumbling', has a plangency and pathos, suggesting that even where the theme is mortality in its undignified, loveless and banal modern settings, the nature of the governing emotion is love, not in personal, romantic form, but universalised as compassion.

2

Elizabeth Bartlett was born in 1924 in Deal, in the mining region of Kent. In 'Betteshanger', a poem which seems to swing between auto-biography and imaginative self-mythologising, she identifies herself as 'one of the pale-faced children of the sea' as opposed to one of those whose fathers 'mucky come to bath / at the end of a shift'. Her mother had worked at one time as a parlour maid. Her father's mother was Irish and had been brought to England as a child during the potato famine. These working-class family origins are modestly explored in a number of poems. Nevertheless, Elizabeth Bartlett has reservations about the working-class label. Of her early life, she writes: 'Yes, it was working-class and it was poor, but it wasn't typical. All my father's sisters and brothers became teachers and two went to university, but as the eldest he missed out on this and, after a spell in the regular army, became a grocer's assistant... My father could well have been a pedantic teacher, but spent his leisure time writing out his life in red exercise books with a stub of pencil...'

Her father seems to have been especially formative in her early-achieved image of herself as someone who would write, 'though nobody, except my mother, would have discouraged me'. Her first ambition was to be a novelist. But the set poetry syllabus of 1935 had a powerful effect. She was delighted by 'Rupert Brooke, of course, and then, mercifully, all the war poets, Owen and Sassoon, in particular, Edward Thomas'. If there is a sense in Bartlett's own work of romanticism saved from itself, it may owe something to Owen's example. Pararhyme for both poets seems a technique of refusing easy consolation.

Despite an early success at the age of nineteen, in Tambimuttu's *Poetry London*, Bartlett did not publish again until her mid-fifties. She left school at fifteen, shortly before the start of the Second World War in 1939, to work in a factory making hypodermic needles. The war itself, early marriage, children and her various jobs in the Home Care Service and as a GP's receptionist, may, to varying degrees, have contributed to the slowing of her poetic career, but nevertheless continued her poetic education by other means. She describes herself as 'not so much a neglected poet as neglectful of the kind of ways to get published at all... It suited me to write without an audience, so that I could do what I wanted without an editor or publisher'. Her output seems to have been small in the 1940s, but subsequently began to build momentum, so that, by the time Harry Chambers of Peterloo Poets approached her in the late 70s with a proposal for a collection, she had a substantial body of work on which to draw. The 80s saw a rapid increase in her output and a steady record of publication. The proliferation of women poets and the delineation of a 'women's poetry' seemed to have proved a stimulus ('for women poets, it's a very exciting time, and it was one hell of a long time coming'). However, she denies having felt any conscious conflict, during the earlier stage of her career, between traditional female roles and the challenge of inventing herself as a poet.

Five years in psychoanalysis were, she feels, crucial to her poetic development. 'I latch on to what I call the neurotic voice,' she writes. 'It has to do with intensity and mood swings, so the language becomes infused with this.' Whether or not, as some feminist critics hold, the woman writer has a particular obligation to make a Persephone-like descent into her own psychic darkness if she is to achieve full artistic integrity. Bartlett's narrators very frequently do make such a descent, and find no easy reassurances there:

> Since you took me by the hand
> and led me to my mother's unmade bed,
> I have waited to be shown this cell,
> the healing physicians opening up wounds,
> guiding me to the peep-hole into hell.
>
> ('The Room')

3

Two Women Dancing contains selections from Elizabeth Bartlett's five published volumes. Though the chronological range in her first collection, *A Lifetime of Dying,* is particularly wide (around 30 years) it was her wish not to present the poems in their chronological order. However, a chronology is appended for readers interested in tracing lines of development.

The selection ends with a gathering of new work that includes the title poem and an extract from the sequence, *Going Home,* based on one of the red notebooks in which her father recorded some of his experiences during the First World War. The volume adds up to a remarkably cohesive yet varied collection by a poet who early discovered her material and her voice, but for whom the immense, often tragic changes in English life this century have been, and continue to be, a source of powerful, angry, distinctive poems.

17

FROM **A LIFETIME OF DYING:**
POEMS 1942-1979 (1979)

Mouths

Mouths are pink tunnels for supermarket food,
For kissing in the dark, out of pity or fear.
A mouth tells us structuralism is all, the lips
Moving, destroying a decade or two in passing.

A mouth is greedy on one breast, an abscess
Forming on the other one. That was the same mouth,
Sucking for dear life, a book propped on his head,
His destiny as clear as a runnel of milky vomit.

How we mouth at each other, like goldfishes
In tanks, eating, kissing, talking, drooping,
Sucking. Sometimes no stiff words creep out
At all. Biting is forbidden. We are not cannibals.

Ah, but mouths can say such words
The heart lurches in its cage, can say words
So compelling there is nothing we would not do
To hear them just once more before we die.

Will the Real William Morris Stand Up?

People need contemporary poetry like a hole in the head.
They need freezers, certainly, and credit cards, mints
With a paralysing flavour, and half-baked bread.

The books they read are found in D.I.Y. shops,
Shaped like bibles and placed upon lecterns.
The wallpaper pages are turned with a correct reverence.
Debate goes on in these high rooms, hourly, daily.

Will the paper match the carpet? Will the carpet
Go with the curtains? It will cost much more
Than the pattern of words we painfully arrange
To paper up the cracks in ruined houses
Full of dripping taps and badly fitting doors.

The pastoral patterns catch the eye.
They will fit in with the stripped pine.
William Morris lives again in flowers not words.
Whoever would stretch out a hand to pluck
Us from the shelves? We should have such luck.

The library, which is next on the list
For Saturday shopping is well-used,
Make no mistake. The whodunnits and biographies
Slide along the glass counters like goods
On an assembly line or pre-packed foods.

Powerful and puny, we stand thin and sickly
Next to *Plays*. Sometimes the date stamp
Doesn't alter from one year to the next.
Thickly crowded we occupy a very small space.
There is no doubt we are undernourished,
Patently unread.

Publishers feed us spoonfuls of patronage,
Magazines allow us the bit the typographer can't use.
We turn hopefully to each other, only to find
The deaf can't hear the deaf, the blind
Can't lead the blind.

Yes, that's the one, the one with everlasting flowers
To decorate the walls which hold us, and wherein
We may lie down to make love and pass the hours
With all the thoughts that poets write about,
And make them ours.

My Five Gentlemen

Prostitutes have clients, wives have husbands,
Poets, you will understand, have editors.
A medieval saint had lice which quietly left him
As his body cooled, their sustenance removed from them.

I have my five gentlemen, one of whom really was
A gentle man, courteous and kind, his rejection slips
Even appeared to be some kind of acceptance,
His face never seen, his care meticulous and honest.

Two was firm and neatly pruned my lines
Like a competent gardener tidying an unwieldy tree.
Faced with mis-spelt, badly typed pages,
He was even provoked into swearing mildly at me.

Three was a witty man, who wrote letters
On a kind of elegant toilet paper, and seen
At a party looked as practised at his social life
As he was at his poetry, though thickening a little.

Four was a shocking surprise. He was not at all
Pretentious. Squinting furtively at him, silent and wary,
I saw this pleasant face, heard a quiet voice, and saw him
Lasting more than a decade or two, a rare animal.

Five is dead, of course. His failing health
Was a comfort to me, though not to him,
Naturally. His death removed one more market
For battered goods, and proved a welcome release.

Rest in peace, I thought (for I always think kindly
Of the gentlemen who direct me to the pages
I am to sit in). I can only hope to be re-cycled
And end up more useful than I would appear to be.

Painting of a Bedroom with Cats

The curved cane chair has dented cushions, the cats
Catch spiders and craneflies on the wardrobe tops,
The guitar lies in its funereal case, the road is quiet,
The apple trees have dropped their fruit in the grass;
Lenin is alive and well and living in Brighton.

The pale watercolour of East Chiltington church
Is crooked on the wall, towels hang like limp flags
On the radiator, the typewriter lid is covered in dust,
The sunflowers are dying in the lime-green mug;
Virginia Woolf is alive and not well and living in Rodmell.

The map of Sussex lies like a large whale among the dolphins
And the coats of arms in a curly formal freckled ocean,
Manuscripts lie like abandoned testaments on the table top,
The bright bedspread is folded neatly at the foot of the bed;
Caxton is alive and well, and living in Bruges.

The fluff stirs under the bed, and the drunks come home,
Singing under the ash tree growing near the iron gate
Which never shuts properly, frail Michaelmas daisies
Glow faintly, a late rose blooms, tattered and mildewed;
Hitler is alive and well and living in Notting Hill.

There is a crack in the ceiling, like the life line on a hand,
A green plant in a pot, but not a pot of basil,
Stands on the loosening tiles, warm empty clothes
Press against each other in the cupboard, like lovers;
Proust is alive and young and living in Combray.

Rain is coming in from the west, the garden is lush and damp,
The drought is over, and the day is at the eleventh hour,
Sleep is nearly here on fern-patterned pillowcases,
Books slither to the floor, cats are stretched on the quilt;
Gwen John is painting a lifetime of dying in a room like this.

Rumours of Wars

My father taught me the tactics of war.
He practised them daily with my mother.
She was always the defeated one, silenced
By his eloquence, his sergeant's ways.

My mother taught me the use of mute insolence,
The correct care of the daily battlefield,
Black-leading stoves, polishing lino and chairs,
Forbidding long hair or fancy clothes and shoes.

My grandmother taught me how to suffer.
'There will be wars and rumours of wars'
She quoted from her bible. I knew that
Already, waiting for skirmishes to start below.

My sister taught me the ammunition of words,
'Liar, pig, cheat, teacher's pet, tell-tale-tit'.
Inadvertently she showed me monthly wounds,
Careless with the concealment of dressings.

My brother taught me that I could commit
Atrocities, forcing him into a dark cupboard,
Telling him of people who pulled small boys
Through the iron gratings over basement windows.

My aunt taught me that great power to charm
And wheedle loving but childless women,
Milking them for money or for favours,
Adept as any politician at a peace treaty.

Soldier's children, we watched our father's
Uniform moulder away, his stories of India
Bored us to tears. Insubordinate kids, we fought
To get out and look for encounters of our own.

Betteshanger

Little Wales beyond England would you call it?
Myfanwy called it the miners' end of town.
We were the pale-faced children of the sea;
They had fathers who mucky came to bath
At the end of a shift. We listened when the light-ship,
Mourning in fog, cried near the Goodwins; they knew
The klaxon call from the mines, accident by fall
Of coal or rush of water. We lay rigid in our
Separate beds, Anglo-Irish and Anglo-Welsh,
Studying Latin and the world of Hollywood,
Where never a miner or a fisherman died,
Just Ginger Rogers and Fred Astaire

Dancing on an endless flood-lit stairway,
Top-hat and tails, no coal in the outhouse,
Or fishscales on their thighs, or money
In tin boxes. Town and gown were never
So apart as we were on the grammar school
Train, uniformed with plaited hair.
Her father, with his blackened muscles
Held my dreams.
Did mine make her walk like the mermaid,
Treading on knives?

Old Movies

The cinema lights are dimmed, the curtains part,
old movies roll back our lives, and now
we sit in the ninepenny seats, eating sweets;
darkness is all around, *Exit only* shows, and *Toilet*
on the other side. The screen, enormous and sensual
reveals the well-groomed girls, the moustached men,
that broad American drawl, those two-tone shoes,
the trilby hats, and call me honey evr' time.

I thought Hollywood was Paradise enough,
for life as she is lived was certainly lived
there, moonlight on balustrades, and the long stare,
the unruffled hair, and the decorous embrace.
We cried a lot, taking our father's handkerchiefs
as Greta Garbo died so elegantly, untouched
by sweat or pain, managing those last few words
with hardly a break, dead in band-box condition,
her lover, neatly suited, distraught with grief
as we were too, hunched in the soft seats,
schoolgirls at a Saturday matinee, learning
about yearning, enrapt until the credits
rolled and we stumbled out, red-eyed
to walk to the bus stop and to home,

to a shared bedroom and a grandmother dying
of cancer in the next room, sweating
and in pain, and the gas-light lowering
as the meter's money ran out yet again.

Front Parlour

There is no way, I know, to see the waters again,
far far out, and a thousand steps to reach the sea.
There is no way back to the ditch he pushed me in
the first day of war, or to smell the musty
cottage he took me to when no bombs fell.
There is no way to hold the first books
in my hand – anti-vivisection, written by a dog,
who described the terrible room in which
he found himself, dog's Dachau, for humans
yet to come, but then, the brave collie
who rescued his friend from the straps
and the cage, and the men in white.
A Victorian shelf, there is not a way
of reconstructing it now, green chenille
curtains and a front parlour, glass vases
and a flecked mirror, and cold linoleum,
a table with brass-clawed feet
which I lay my hot cheek against.
There is no going back, only forward,
surrounded by things as unlike
that special room as I know how.
Why, if there is no way back,
do I hear the dogs howl, the curtains clash
on the brass pole, the sea
splash far out, and distant,
and the hard body pinning me down
in the September ditch,
as the sirens wailed.

Neurosis

I am a dark cypress driven in the wind,
And the quarrelling voices of children behind
The Sunday streets. I am the listener, waiting
In doorways for the sounds of struggle
And torment. I am the shock machine in the empty ward,
And the enemy soldier under the point of the sword.
I am a little boy crying out Dolore in his sleep,
And the dazed women in rusty black who weep
Outside provincial cemeteries, and a foetus taken piecemeal
From its mother, and an old woman dying
Of cancer in a back room. I am my own analyst lying
Dead in his bed with the marks of the syringe
Like a macabre tattoo on his white body.

In childhood I was the red lady of my own nightmares,
And the pursuing jeers, and the hostile stares.
I was Manuela dead in a German courtyard, and the open maw
Of the butcher boy's basket, and the threat of war.
I was the clinging Goodwins who sucked down the merry
Cricketers, and the drums at the tattoo, and the poisoned berry.
Did you see me lingering at the gates of Buchenwald,
Or running from Electra, or making friends with the bald
Syphilitic hawking laces on the sea-front?
I was all men collecting the dole in long lines
In bitter weather, and the accident siren shrieking from the mines.
You have heard my name called in the courts
Of law for perversion and murder, and malice aforethought.

Would you know me? I am also a young woman, growing
My flowers in season, feeding my cats, knowing
Little, but feeling everything, writing at all times
And in all places, working out rhythms and rhymes.
I make clothes for young children, a red kilt
Or a jacket for a newly-delivered child,
Assuaging my envy and covering my guilt.
Sometimes, from my husband's arms, I catch
A glimpse of the potency of love, like a mirage
Soon gone, and I wonder if I shall ever be whole,
Or always playing torturer and tortured in my double role.

Design

The blanched eyes of the aspens
Quiver at the field's edge, their mad cascades
Of butterflies turn swift and brittle,
A swirling precision of whites and jades,
Like notes in a sick brain, the beat
Of Ravel
Dying in a Parisian clinic,
Between white walls in a tree-lined street.

This summer field bears the weight
Of the brassy buttercups,
And the bodies of you and me
As we lie down together.
The field is as bright as the sands
Of Saintes-Marie-de-la-Mer,
Or the chair
Of the madman of Arles.

Southover

French rolls I bought, running
Velvet-slippered, humming
Bach, on cool October mornings
In the nineteenth year.

A marriage bed I found, dancing
A swift primeval dance
Between laundered sheets. Young
I was, and the tune difficult
To follow, many-melodied
Like Bach.

Calm walls I had, wooden floors
And painted windows watching
A leaf-strewn road; no trousseau

And a leaping-shadowed ceiling
At my consummation.

Crazy music I heard, cacophony
Of colour and breath, and spindleberries
In a pale grave jar,
A back cloth
To my strange triumphant silences.

A lover I had, clear-voiced
And double-lived, like Bach.
He walked
About my rooms, an unexplained
Hypnotic walk; he touched
My breasts, and lit a fire
In my house,
And in me.

The Child Is Charlotte

Wish me out of this coma of fantasy
Into which I have fallen, and lie
Floating and submerged by turns,
Pacing the paths with Charlotte
In my arms. The die
Is cast against me, the burns
Wrinkle on my arms, the symbols
Of all that may make or mar a child,
And the child is Charlotte.

The drifting shawl severs the dead
Twigs in the dream's edge, the forceps
Fail, the blessings deceive us,
All is broken and lost in the oncoming
Dusk, in the oncoming head.
Who will receive us,
When we are separate,
After the pain has been ridden,
After the incubus returns unbidden?

I have so little to give you,
Only the tedious knot of pain,
No sooner unravelled than knotted again,
A faltering facility with words,
A mountain from my molehill's feeling.
A deft hand to spin your name
In the fall of a peeling.
No love, if my own love gutters and dies,
And the darkness rushes in.

Paltry the gifts for Charlotte, no magi
Travelling the interminable wastes
For a new-born child, only
Implacable genes, uncertain myrrh
For so long a season. The lonely
Gold is no reward for her,
Death being no solution for a wayward child,
Grown weary with waiting, grown wild
With anguish, and the child is Charlotte.

All we have for the moulded head
Unmeshed, is our own particular web
Of mingling and unformulated beliefs,
And the varying means by which we live,
The blunt fingers on a recorder,
The poetry written with difficulty
Between supper and sleep, a retinue
Of cats, to have and to keep, all
Their nine lives, many-covered books
Longed for, to suck and chew upon,
Being nearest to hand, but forbidden
Always.

Here is your bubble, my bountiful.
Here is your room.
Here to excrete and vomit and bloom
Like a rose.
Here is my womb
Clinically correct.
I hope you may never know
The reluctance
Of this blossoming turmoil.

Who do we think we are, to engender this life,
To set it stumbling forward, out into those passions
Of fear and mistaken ecstasy, down darkening years,
Reproachful, as we have been reproachful? Fashions
Change, wars divide and split the world,
Childhood is gone, the body buds and breaks,
Blooms, deteriorates, trembles, grows old,
Grows still, is bundled away, lies
In a coffin covered with sacking
On some remote railway platform.
Who are we to lie like gods on a cotton quilt,
Listening to the spread of rain through stem
And root and layer of soil, and from the dregs of guilt
And distaste bring forth this infant, this old woman,
This child called Charlotte.

Birth

When they gave you to me you were redolent
Of acrid badly-made soap and blood,
And indeed you were covered with a waxy layer,
Like rice-paper on a macaroon, or cottage cheese.
You had obviously done some very heavy laundry
In the womb, using soda, wringing your hands,
Purple and sodden like a washer-woman,
Whose feeble fingers have mandarin's nails
With which you scratched your face, adding
To the general air of wear and tear and age.
And yet you were so young, a few minutes,
And the placenta not yet flowering in the bowl,
Your doll's clothes still airing, your air-way
Choked with mucus. All night we drained
You like a boiled potato, tipping you up
And, newly-washed we looked upon your great
High forehead, and your thin crop of hair,
And marvelled that you had travelled so far
Through such a small tunnel, no cuts,
No stitches, no forceps, just a long journey

And a small body, like a fish, sliding neatly
Into a quiet house, and an old bed,
Where no other child had been born before.
You cried a little, and then, exhausted, fell
Into the deepest sleep there is, apart
From death, and I lay flat and empty
Awake all night, tired beyond sleep,
Fearing and hoping beyond all bounds
That you would not live to curse your birth
As many have done before you,
And will do again.

Loving Neighbour

This summer, the unfamiliar sea, and the driftwood
Leaning against the wall in the sun, and the pile
Of kindling grown too big, because the letter says work,
Because the letter says stoop and carry,
Drag the wood from the cargo ships a mile
Over the rocks, and you may miscarry.

The sea has deprived the happy pregnant women
Of their golden oranges. They rot in the sand
Among the broken crates and the twisted branches,
And the bloated life-belts under this sultry
Summer sky, but the letter says work, do not stand
And think, but work, and cancel out adultery.

These long weeks the sea has been too calm,
The sun too bright and regular to hold my pain.
Even the letter says storm and the waves beating,
For the letter says work, and the storm brings wood,
And flings it along the shore, bright paint and salt stain,
Pattern and chaos, and sodden food.

Tonight, the bell-buoy out in the bay,
And the gulls' feet pattering on the tiles:
And the path to the sands trodden hard,

And the house swept clean, because I may not marry.
But the letter says get up, add to the pile
Of kindling, and you may miscarry.

I do not know why the gulls are silent,
There is no colour in the sea and the sands are empty and clean.
In my belly your storm advances,
But my mind is as calm as this strange sad summer has been.

Where is my loving neighbour? Who will help me to bed?
The sea is my loving neighbour, and the sand shifts under my head.
No one gathers driftwood by moonlight,
But I have done what the letter said.

David In Roma

David in Roma, under the gilded tree,
Turns a pale face to me,
From a Christmas which has gone,
But is here always.
Photographed in Roma, forever forlorn,
Forever four years old, he
Looks out coldly, grown
Grave and remote, sitting alone
Hand upon knee, then, now,
Under the bough
Of his Christmas tree.

Now in the streets of Rome the children run,
Now in Regents Park the creak of hoop, the click of gun,
And the bleating doll cries ma-ma, spinning a cry
Between London and Rome, faster than his aeroplane can fly,
Cries ma-ma ma-ma under the frowning sky,
Between the naked trees, along the paths, here where no sun
Breaks through, and there, where the children run
With David in Roma.

Is the spring early in Rome?
Tell me, does the dome
Of St Peter's shine like the dome
Of St Pauls?
For you, the morning walk
Must be taken somewhere; but not here,
And the games and the talk
Must be in one language or another,
Out in the street, out in the via,
At one time or another,
There or here

No one walks in the park when the sour fog swirls.
This is no weather for boys and girls
To come out to play at birth and death; the child
Who dies on the green battlefields of St Pancras, the child
With a baby for each lived year, like a mild
Victorian mama, feeling the china skull beneath the curls;
They are all at home till the grass is dry and the fog unfurls,
Like a day in Roma.

David in Roma, David in Rome,
David in London, David at home,
Over the mountain and over the sea,
The Pope can dance with my Lady Lee.
O-U-T spells out,
And out goes he.

No Rain on Campus

In the formal nineteenth-century parkland
The university buildings rise like glass palaces;
The young men have long hair. They look like princes,
Or like Rossetti, whose vacant house I used to pass
On the Kent coast when I was a child on holiday.
They look careless and young, definite and vociferous –
No eight-till-six in a hypodermic needle factory
As I did when I was younger than I am now.

One pushes a pamphlet into my hand. *No rain on campus*
Is the curious slogan I read, duplicated on purple paper,
A crude drawing of a monster swallowing a child.
Solve your crèche problems. Throw your children
To the animals. The monster has the look of a benign dinosaur
Made in the sixties with assorted plastic pieces
By a small child, not thinking he would join
The princes, the hem of his denim trousers
Dragging in the dust, and his hair flowing free
As a drowning maiden. *Picton is semi-divine*,
I read. Alas, poor Picton, who is he?
Hail Mary, mother of student, who am I,
Who dug no waste land on Margate sands,
Only a castle pocked with shells and deep with dungeons?
Like a mystical message I carry it with me,
Seeming for a while like the words of the man
Who walked with trousers rolled by the sea,
A young man in a dry month, waiting for rain,
But here, no rain, no rain, *no rain on campus*.

God Is Dead – Nietzsche

Daddy and I are always here, you know,
Whenever you want us.
We didn't like the things you said
The last time home.
Bourgeois, you said, and a word which sounded
Very like atrophied.
Daddy doesn't like the way you collect
Toilet graffiti,
God is dead – Nietzsche, and the reply,
Nietzsche is dead – God.

You can't expect Daddy to go round
With the plate in church
With thoughts like that in his head.
I worry too.
Structuralism sounds like a building-site,

Semiology sounds rather rude
In a medical kind of way.
The dogs are well, both almost human,
As we've often said
To you.

Please wear a vest, the days are getting
Colder. We hope you will not be so rude
The next time home.
Daddy and I have just re-done your room.
The blood on the wall hardly shows
After two coats of paint.
Cambridge must be very pretty just now.
I am, in spite of everything,
Your loving Mother.

Lisson Grove

After I left you, a thin vapour settled on my mind.
I walked past the rubber shops and the urinals.
I walked past the shop with the dusty 1910 shoes.
I walked past the crowding basements, the blinds
Were crookedly hung, the plants faded, broken,
The kids were yelling from first-floor windows,
All summer stunned and bleeding in Paradise,
In the vomit-stained rotting courts of Paradise.

After I left you, words would not hang upon feelings.
Grief, parting, goodbye, never. O God, O Lisson Grove.
I walked past the open door of the church, and incense
Was flung out at me like a rotten cabbage. Come,
Said the virgin and all the tatty saints, come, come.
Come, said the skin-and-bone Christ and his seven-foot cross,
But I walked past, dragging my own cross behind me,
Each step bruising my heels as it lurched behind me.

After you left me, the sun wavered and dimmed in the sky.
I saw a negress in a mauve cardigan picking her bad teeth.

I saw a grey lace curtain twitch as I sidled past.
I saw black hair-combings twined on a rusty railing,
A clot of blood blooming in the road like a peony,
And scrawled chalk genitals on a subway wall,
Like a message of primitive magic now lost to me,
And you, packed and gone and laid away, now lost to me.

After you left me, images obscene and sorrowful
Followed the jerking hearse of our un-natural love.
On a coffin of couches I lay down and wept for us,
And for the feet which walked in the 1910 shoes,
And the dolled-up virgin's swollen uterus,
And the mourning face behind the curtain,
And the hand which held the chalk, alone, in the dark,
And your hand which turned on the gas, alone in the dark.

Disposing of Ashes

A grey day in June, as cold as charity,
The full-leaved trees sinister in heavy green,
The undertaker wearing his winter coat.
Our cold lies inside us like a cube of ice
Unmelting in the core of our being,
Untouched by succeeding summers,
For June will always be cold now,
However bright the sun, however fragmented
The light and shade, the overblown rose,
The tall grasses seeding in a recession,
The tar bubbling on the hot roadways.
Death stamps its mark on a month
And a year. Never will Jubilee tat
Be a joke any more. Sodden bunting
Hangs in the rain, swags and crowns
Disintegrate. Only the plastic flags
Survive, flapping disconsolately on fences
And front doors. It has been a wet week,
The street parties were a wash-out,
The public junketing an offence against

Private grief. Even Ditchling Beacon
Looks menacing, and the ashes not soft
As in imagination, but like pellets
Almost. We dump them among the rabbit
Droppings, and run through the mud
And drizzle, back to nothing
Where something was before,
Leaving our royal one soaking
Into the soft downland grass
Faceless to the sky.

There Is a Desert Here

I loved you in silence, without hope, jealous and afraid.
PUSHKIN

There is a desert here I cannot travel,
There is sand I cannot tip from my shoes.
Over my left eyebrow is a greenish bruise.
There is you, and there is me. I cannot choose
But love you, though you wrong me,
And make angry love to me, a smack
Like a caress, a careless move, and a crack
Appears in your loving, widening, widening.
It was a bad bargain I made with you.
Your green eyes and your strutting maturity
Did not mix well with my long pale face
And my convent innocence, but they looked
At me, flashes of light, like sexual lightning,
Blackening my tree. At last I sprout
From the bole after all these years
When you might have thought my tears
Were gone, and my tortured tree was dead.

Come, little creatures, walk on me,
Come, little worms, slide upon me,
For no man ever will again.
I watched beetles and ladybirds
Long before you gathered birch twigs

To beat me in a field – in fun, of course,
And I will watch them again,
And grow old ungracefully, barefoot
And sluttish in my ways.
No more hauling of ashes,
I promise you.

A Wrong Kind of Levitation

Trying out the kind of levitation he had suggested,
the Sussex fields lay variegated, rounded, diverse
as the marks on a tortoise-shell cat, a map like
an untidy chess board, the pawns capturing kings
and queens, the bright flocks of clouds pulling
at her hair. On to the mosaic of the Surrey hills
the cracked and crazy voices talked of lynchets,
bridle paths, foxes panting in their hidden earths,
the rain in a mizzle and a flurry stung her cheeks,
bloodless though they were, incorporeal, transparent,
down the alleys and tunnels of the freezing winds.

He had asked originally for various parts of her,
a small toe or an ear, a strand of straight hair.
Ethereal and tenuous, the wrong parts, tear filled
eyes, her hands like lizard's paws, tactile sensations,
entangled on the wooded slopes, lost somewhere in Kent,
somehow a wrong turning, somewhere a faulty diagram.
Stretched on her airy rack, she would not take
back the painful spasms, and, killed by inches,
severed herself, to re-assemble in a place
by a river, bruised but whole, quietly creeping
up the stairs to where he sat alone in his room.

It had all been a joke, he said, willing her breasts
like pale lighted globes at a children's party.
That was all he meant. It had all been for nothing,
that thermal riding where the owls called out at night,
and all the strident country noises, creak and squeak

and scream were like the howling of her separation.
Sitting crouched over other people's lives and lines,
and clearing a space among the papers and the books
he made a perfect jigsaw of her organic parts
and sent her home alone, kissing her lips as he
pressed them into position, opening the windows wide.

He worked alone each evening. Her clinging intensity
scared him stiff. Presented with this Brontë wraith
he regretted the sci-fi appearance of what had been
a harmless joke, to please his own need to feel
and touch, this mental and spiritual contact he was
always talking of. Her scattered witch-like ride
made him wonder what the hell he'd let himself in for,
sat her on his knee, vainly chafed her cold body,
and her thin white arms like ectoplasm at a seance,
which enfolded him too tightly for his comfort,
let her go with relief, reached for a glass and drank.

I Am That E

I don't appear on the pages
Very often now. At first,
Like a new toy, I was played with,
Seduced among the ferns, ravaged,
Defeated, and wildly praised.
I played the awkward role
Of stepmother to two fair-haired
Children, fair like their indiscreet
Mother. I wrote some poetry here
And there. Published here and there,
Mostly without payment or much reward.
Now, I see the country as your bride.
Among the budding groves, and trees
You are yourself, as your father was,
Watching the woods and fields, finding
Such infinite variety as no woman
Can provide.

This is the time of year, you write,
When little boys go away to school
And old men die, and wives give birth.
Your children, your father, your wives,
And one sad Austrian mistress
Whom you left for me,
You would barter them all
For a cloud or a tree.
We parted long ago, but still
We live together, and my dark-haired
Child walks by the river Cam,
With his head as full of words
As yours and mine, not knowing
A willow from an ash,
Or his father from me.

Now I appear as a figure, part house-keeper,
Part sexless menopausal creature, an interior
Person, surrounded by my urban garden,
Still afraid of the bleak downs and villages,
Cherishing my cats, lying in my mother's
Coffin, with her quiet voice and grave eyes,
Working where she might have lived,
Walking the bare brown corridors,
Surrounded by old people's trash and tittle,
Kissing their cheeks when I leave,
Like embracing a leper, I sometimes feel.
You are free to go far away into untouched places,
I go into imprisoned lives, imprisoned myself,
For I am that E.

Corpus Christi

This is the only decaying nineteenth-century house with a stable
      block
Left smong the ranks of square boxes with small gardens covered
      with grass
And with central heating, a shower, a colour TV, and two-car
      garage,
And a mortgage high enough to preclude the price of a literary
      evening class.

42

In the stable block, which lies well behind the stone pillared
        portico,
There is no heating, and a jagged hole in the faded flowered
        wallpaper.
Since some well-heeled family lived out their lives secluded in this
        house
Leading out their horses on to the uneven mossy bricks we pick
        our way across
Every Wednesday at eight, it was a receiving place for children in
        care,
And now a tarted-up Adult Education Centre with plastic chairs
        in the main hall.

Some places carry their past with them, and this place is one of
        those.
The tears that were shed the first lonely night here, seep slowly
        through
The old traditional ballads we are reading now, cruel mothers so
        far back
They were not read about but told and re-told, or chanted and
        sung,
The dead returning with the birch bark on their hats, the children
        returning
From some bedsit in Wandsworth, or some grimy institutional
        hostel room.

Ballads are full of the babies born on the wrong side of the
        blanket,
As many of these must have been, led up these stairs, the un-
        familiar name
Of stable block as incomprehensible as the kindly, over-worked
        staff
Who sent them to bed without a comforting packet of chips, or
        herded them
Out into the vast gardens to play and chant those rhymes which
        have such links
With the ballads we earnestly listen to on a faulty tape-recorder
        tonight,
The violent cryptic stories so like the horror comics the bold ones
        smuggled
In, not understanding Beatrix Potter, or Arthur Ransome with his
        special children.

These children were special too. Dead father. Sick mother.
        McCrimon is gone,
Is gone, he will never come back, he will never come back, he is
        gone;
Quavering in Gaelic, the singer's cracked old voice uses her notes
        like a wail.
Corpus Christi I think I shall choose for next week's chilly session,
Feeling a wounde that is always bledyng as they lie upon their
        beds,
With comics under their pillowes and nits in their little heds.
Their hearts are surely turned to ston, Corpus Christi wretyn
        thereon.

Ian, Dead of Polio

How old were you, Ian?
I was six and I lay
On a hot bed, hearing
The thin spidering shouts
Along the suburban roads,
Flying among the prunus
Trees, and dying behind
The front doors of Fairview,
The Haven, Guerison.

What were you like, Ian?
I was a fat child,
With fair hair,
And I would have become
A fat business man
In the city perhaps,
Or on the road,
Travelling in corsets,
Or natty kitchenware.

How did you die, Ian?
I died in a clean hospital,
Hot and tired and clamped
Into an iron box, like a beetle
In a matchbox. I saw
Mama when the tall
And turgid dreams burst
And fell about me,
And I was afraid.

Have you anything to say, Ian?
I want to say
That I was sick
And my head ached,
But it did not change
Into a toy on the bed,
Or a cup of milk spilt
On the sheet,
And a lightly boiled egg.

It changed into death
And delirium and spiralling
Dark, and a smiling gentleman
In black, and Mama gone.

This was an ordinary child who fled
From the semi-detached houses,
And television at five,
Who died, either in the sterile darkness of the ward,
At the age of six, or on the road to Leeds, cardboard
Boxes of corsets heaped on the worn back seat, at the age of sixty
Half in a ditch and smelling of whisky.

In Memory of Steve Biko

Somehow the drains of feeling were blocked that week.
Biko died, and also a giraffe called Victor who was thought
To be mating at the time, and fell and couldn't get up again.
For Biko, also, it was a fall into death, the cause

Unknown, but guessed at, something far more disturbing
Than a very large animal, hauled to his feet, and perhaps
One day to be stuffed. We all know who hogged the news,
A simple but prolonged death, a pretty girl keeper,
Not a young black man.

We who mourned him were not the giraffe mourners,
And we measure with our eyes the space he died in,
And the means that brought his life to an end,
And the fact that good does not triumph over evil,
If indeed it ever did. Cradled in soft arms
With a girl's hair on his cheek he would never
Have believed his luck, but thought it one more
Trick in a diabolical game of cards.
Steve Biko, the sweet voice cries, lie here
Against this bale of straw. You were said
To have died on hunger strike
But this was not the case.

There will obviously be very little left
Of you to stuff as a memorial in King Williams Town,
And your mating days are over now;
All your days are over now, for good and all.

As the news came in the following weeks
It seemed he died, as they say, under interrogation,
Said to have laughed at his keepers, said to have
Died of brain damage, naked and manacled.
He was careless enough to have injured himself,
Or so it would appear. The animal died
Like a man, the man like an animal,
As the drains of feeling gradually unblocked,
The canvas hoists were folded away,
The manacles were shown in the courts.
No one was to blame, was the verdict.

In two minutes flat.

Farewell, Gibson Square

(for Dr Susan Heath)

We did surgeries together. I warned her
Who liked litigation, and who were devious,
And who were mildly insane.
We managed to break a patient's arm
Between us, when he fell unconscious
To the floor. In the surgery,
I ask you, what shame. True the patient
Was deaf, and didn't hear our questions;
Compassion ended in gusts of laughter.
Not seemly. She wasn't a seemly girl,
Newly qualified, tat became her;
She wasn't sure if medicine
Was her thing. Lying in bed, smoking,
And reading, was. She taught me
How to pour a Guinness slowly;
She was pale and slow-spoken, witty
And thin.
Hospitals got her down, she said,
After a while, that is,
And furnished rooms made her puke,
But pubs and jumble sales
Were her natural habitat.
At last I heard she'd got a job
In a chest clinic, smoking illicitly
In the toilets, no doubt.
Fair Susan, with your Afro hair-style,
Your pot-plants, and your miniscule
Bank balance, I miss you.
Professional boredom has settled in
Again, and patients go home whole.

Immunisation Day

Some sit pale and scared, not touching the comics,
Waiting their turn, silent and tense. They are the ones
Who know about pain, but do not cry, frozen like rabbits
In their tracks. We, the predators, fill up syringes
Talking of jabs with the carelessness of a weekly chore.
Once in a while one child flies round the room, moth-like,
Screaming. We, the giants, grab him, hold him down,
And the wings fold, he is carried out, stuffed with sweets,
Sees us in his dreams at night, knocks against the trolley.
Last of all comes the survivor, who bares his own arm,
And when it's over says with distaste and severe honesty
'You hurt me. That bloody hurt, that did.' We recognise
The others, but he disconcerts us, and he kicks the door
As he goes out, leaving a mark like a scratch on white skin.

Safe

*Incest is common in large families, both mother and daughter conniving
in keeping the father satisfied, with payment as part of the deal.*
SOCIAL WORKER'S REPORT

The father pays his dues. Once dandled on his knee
She now lies down to receive him obediently.
At first she cried, but thought the money easily won,
Dreamed of other things while he laboured above her,
His eyes seeing the likeness to her mother, the same
Hair, the same turning away. Enraged by this sometimes
He hit her. The mark faded by Monday, and the school
Was so large, a slight weal on a girl's cheek
Went unremarked.

The mother lies alone in the back bedroom, her fist
Clenched as she hears the same slap she once kissed
Away, but now tries to forget, shifting her heavy body,
Enduring her prolapsed womb, wiping her sweating face.
Sometimes when the social worker comes she betrays

Unease, drops a cup. Hot flushes multiply like weals
Upon her face. There is something in this house which
A trained mind senses, but silence is all she receives,
There is nothing untoward.

The daughter likes the weekdays. All the lively boys
Who followed her out of the womb laugh and make a noise
In their communal room. She dreams of a sister
Who would have taken alternate weeks perhaps, sharing
The burden of his drunken body and her mother's
Pale secrecy. He penetrates her deeper than she knows,
For all her men and even her sons will have a look
Of him, and they will all complain how quiet she is,
Avoiding the neighbours.

The social worker writes out her notes, yawning her way
To bed: Leary, B., navvy of Irish extraction. Leary, J.,
Menopausal, depressed; girl, sixteen, six boys, overcrowding:
Reports on the Leary boys, wild, cheeky, smoking already,
Nicking cigarettes, out late, truanting from school.
Leary, Mary, a quiet girl in stylish clothes, with fine
Long hair, attends school regularly, stays at home
On Saturday nights. At least, she thinks, one child here
Is safe from harm.

The Visitors

This patient was obviously hallucinating as I spoke to her.
CONSULTANT'S NOTE

There was one in the room, thinking of the sherry
he would have before lunch, rocking slightly in his chair.

There was another opposite him, grey hair falling
across a face like a coy but ravaged schoolgirl.

There were others present to whom she would have talked
had he not asked her tedious questions, eyeing her.

They were invisible to him, his ego balanced well,
his libido functioning perfectly, his accountant satisfied.

Sometimes their faces got between her and the desk,
mocking and bony, whispering foul insinuations.

When they advanced too far across the carpet
she wanted to get up and tell them to go away,

but his tight clinical voice held her poised
between the overt grins and the beckoning hands.

In the end, he won, and the others bobbed like balloons
in a corner, unmistakably there, but further away.

At last she was compelled to tell them to go away from her,
though she could see them reflected in his glasses, waiting.

He asked her questions, and noted down her hesitant answers
in a precise hand on a long yellow form.

In the end, he formally ushered her out into the corridor,
the faces, mouthing obscenities, followed in a muddled bunch,

crowding with her through the narrow door, escorting
her back to the ward where they settled in like squatters,

one on the end of the bed, some by the locker,
and one who laid his head on her pillow, talking softly

until she fell asleep abruptly, and for a while
the visitors crept away silently or floated gently out,

leaving only the faintest trace of their presence,
like a perfume or a discarded cigarette burning away.

Surgery

On my desk lies an informative leaflet about Lassa fever,
And also a note on which is scrawled 'Can the doctor come.
Mum is poorly again, and oblige, yours truly. P.S.
Can't phone, box not working.' My phone rings,
And 'nocte', I write, 'two tabs, mare 1 tab, 10mg',
And answer the call at the same time. If I sound distant,
So does she – South Africa maybe, bleeding in Soweto,
But no, she has a sort of headache, and no, she cannot
Come this morning, because she's having her hair done.
Tonight perhaps, when the whole circus starts again,
The lion roars, the clown feigns dead, the tent
Shudders in the wind, the patients applaud.

The post is waiting to disgorge a message of hope
At last destroyed, an X-ray form with a fatal shadow,
Or N.A.D., those divine initials to say there's nothing wrong,
No abnormality detected. Before I have time to remember
The warm bed I left an hour ago, from a mystical erotic dream
I only half recall, the surgery begins in earnest.
Some cough, some limp, some sit and gaze, and one small child
Runs in and out, so plump of cheek, red of lip, blue of eye,
And full of energy, he removes the S-TI ticket
From my Caligari filing-cabinet. If he were taller
Would he snatch the A-BA with his neat questing squirrel paws
Indifferent to where he is? He might, but half way through
The morning and half way through the post, I tear up a few
Drug company ads. Maybe I've ditched a miracle drug, or
Another thalidomide. Who knows?

I have unpacked the vaccines and laid out the syringes,
And listed the house-calls, street by street, house by house,
When I see him standing at the door, gaunt and dignified,
Wearing a look of such suffering that even the squirrel
Runs to his mother and buries his face in her trousered lap.
He is a terminal case, and knows it, but he comes each week,
And for a moment, detachment deserts me. I want to cry,
Come here, my love, and I will save you. I will kiss and comfort
You, and bring you strawberries out of season, and wine
In a silver goblet, and deliver you from all pain and sorrow.
Come into the dream I left before I came this morning,
Briskly unlocking the door on another day, another surgery.

The Old Workhouse

It's very cosy here. Some kind and misguided person
Has carefully made garish curtains with yellow roses
And put them up at the workhouse windows. Of course
We don't call it that now. This is our geriatric ward.
No, Maggie, you can't go home today, not ever
Maggie, not ever, but you don't know it yet.
Somewhere, in this frenzied pacing she knows this.
She knows the end, as dumb creatures know the smell
Of the abattoir, falling on their knees under the blow,
Ready for the well-kept tables of hotels and *pensions*,
Their flesh laid out on decorative plates, the wine
Blood red on the right hand, the waiters discreetly hovering.

It's at the back of beyond, the reluctant visitors say,
And she doesn't know me when I come, so what's the use.
She thinks I'm her sister Flo and when she wets
The polished floor she thinks it is the waters of the Usk
Where once she paddled as a child, the water
Cool and fresh, not warm and disgraceful. (Enter
An auxiliary downstage left with bucket and mop,
And disinfectant.) Everyone pretends it hasn't happened,
Except Maggie, who quietly weeps and asks again
To go home, away from this dreadful lunatic place
She doesn't remember being brought to, and from which
Dick would take her, if only he were alive.

Richard and Margaret they were then, somewhere about 1900.
She was a slender girl with a devoted young husband,
Who wanted her to have the best of everything, a car,
A house of their own, a joint on Sunday, a spin in the country.
When they retired they bought a bungalow in Sussex,
And no children sullied their well-kept rooms
For they never had either, only each other, and a Daimler.
One November day he died, stretched out on the kitchen floor.
The neighbours ran hurriedly across the neat front lawn,
Treading in mud which she carefully cleaned away
After the ambulance had gone and she'd phoned her friends,
Shocked that he'd left her to live out her life alone.

The country here is flat and ordinary, the trees
Seem aware that their purpose is to screen the old workhouse,
And not to grow in glory, as even the trees in municipal parks
Manage to do, sheltering lovers and children and old men
Still free to sit upon the benches in the sun and gossip.
This is not Dachau, don't be absurd. We do our best
To make the old folk happy, even if staff are a problem,
Coloured, and do not understand the language of the dying.
We prefer to call it their last home, and put them to bed
At six, well-drugged and out of the way, and quiet.
Hark how the Daimler's wheels hiss on the drive outside,
As Maggie goes forth like a queen, waving her last goodbye.

Polling Station

This park is a curious place,
Ravishing in the moonlight, the trees
Like iron scrolls against the autumn sky.
Day reveals the dog turds crumbling
Into a fine dust, the graffiti on the walls
Of the cricket pavilion, the tennis courts
With wire as high as Buchenwald behind
Our backs.
This is our polling station for today.
The man I am telling with says that Spain
Is the place to go, the streets orderly;
The prisons full, I think, but do not say.
He went to the Costa Brava and ate his chips
With the rest of them. Our rosettes are different,
But we take the voters' numbers for knocking up.
I think I hear the knock on the door
In another country, another time, another climate.
I hear them screaming in the streets
Of Guernica, or marching sadly and wearily
Cloth-capped from Jarrow, my father's
Meetings in the front parlour, my mother's distaste
For the fag-ends afterwards.
There is no chance in this constituency for us,

There never was, and the polling station stands
On the right side of the park where the houses have names
And drives, instead of numbers and back alleys.
L'Étranger, I am always on the wrong side,
For the wrong reason, in the wrong place.
This park is a curious place. I am oddly comforted
By the boarded-up windows of the pavilion,
The empty Coke bottles rolling down the steps.
This is the place the aimless young frequent
On any other day, leaving their writing on the wall.
They do not come from the detached houses
Any more than I did. Inside this earnest
Provincial lady a young rebel cries to be released,
But she completes her list and then walks away
Across the park, back to Camus, unfinished,
Lying broken-backed at page two hundred,
Back to the cats lying entwined on the Spanish bedspread.
They would, of course, vote on both sides,
Always there for extra rations, never for extra work.
In the morning the battle is finished, the dogs take over,
The kids sprawl where the voters trod the day before.

W.E.A. Course

This evening we are doing Pasternak.
Last week we did Alexander Solzhenitsyn.
Outside this room which has wall to wall carpets
And stands illuminated in its own grounds,
The English autumn dies, modest and well-mannered,
The leaves swept away from the drive, the sun still warm
During the daylight hours, warmth reflected upon the face
Of our tutor, who could be my son, and looks like
D. H. Lawrence.
They should have warned me of Simochka
Who sits on my right in fashionable clothes,
And long blond hair, or Nerzhin,
Who was transferred at the end of chapter nine.

We sit in a circle, but Dante would not have recognised us
As persons with grave and tranquil eyes and great
Authority in our carriage and attitude.
This proves we have actually read *The First Circle*,
But this week I am glad to have travelled
The long train journey without Omar Sharif,
And seen the candles burn, and the iced rowanberries.
Across the room sits Lara, rather silent and also
A librarian, and next to her the Public Prosecutor.
Outside the wind is blowing, and the snow blocks out
This commuter town, silting against the door.
We are trapped, we cannot escape, we grovel
For a few potatoes, a few logs of wood.
Red specks and threads of blood gleam on the snow,
And the sound of gun-fire ends the class as we flee
In cars and on bicycles with our books under our arms.
Next week to Sicily with Lampedusa,
Nunc et in hora mortis nostrae. Amen,
And I shall be cast for the Leopard's wife,
Gesummaria, how far away the snow will seem.
It will be hot wherever we are, and Bendico
Will follow me home through the neon-lighted streets,
His dust will crumble and his smell pursue me,
As Komarovsky pursues me now, in his green car,
Dark as the forests at Varykino, cold as a Russian
Winter, in this Michaelmas weather, cruel and ruthless
As the unseasonable revolution we are all waiting for,
With only a grammar of feeling to defend us.
Ah, Yury, the snow is falling, the stars have gone,
And I am alone; we are lost to each other forever.

Degrees

We are the ones with Fabergé's eggs
concealed about our persons, or walking
humpty-dumpty up the ante-natal clinic path.
No doubt you wish we were not here at all,
gazing out over the heads of sleeping children
at the boxes which are our homes, and gardens
full of prams and strung with washing lines.

We are the ones who don't appear too much,
the ones which modern English poetry
could do without. We don't hold degrees,
except perhaps of feeling, the mercury
shooting up and down like crazy.
Oh lord, the thermometers we break,
the sweaty sheets in which we lie awake!

We have no O levels, or A levels either.
We didn't fight and we didn't win,
we only ran to get the washing in.
Look out, you just missed us
as you crossed the crowded campus.
We were only there to clean the floors
and hand your morning coffee out.

FROM **STRANGE TERRITORY**
(1983)

Strange Territory

What am I doing here? I only know
the landscapes of back streets, small
houses behind whose doors lie the full
commodes, the scattered crumbs, tins
of soup, pale faces of the prisoners,
and gardens where ox-eye daisies, ling
and feathered grasses conquer everything.

England, England, Lindfield's pest house,
Eastaway's rigor mortis monkey-puzzle tree,
the sad occupants of terminal stations,
dressed like Morris men with newspapers
tied round their legs, arguing endlessly
with themselves, the old lags writing
poetry which rhymes but is not exciting.

No ordnance survey map depicts the things
etched behind my eyes, the mortician's room,
where he lays out the tools of his trade,
the cotton wool to puff out cheeks, a stitch
inserted in the mandible, the lipstick (pink
for babies), and the tape to bind together
autopsy cases. He works fast in hot weather.

Like snow on fells where I have never been,
he dusts powder onto unresisting cheeks,
plugs the anus, receives best suits, nightgowns
and Babygros for babies who will not grow
any bigger. The women may even have kept
their wedding dresses. His wife lets seams
in and out, his willing preserver of dreams.

Strange territory this. The rivers are full
of blood, the inhabitants are criminals
or old or dead, the routes are arteries marked
with cottages, rusting kitcheners, disposable
sheets; the valleys are dark as shadows
in tenement yards, and only the sky is as wide
as your arms or the length of your stride.

Autumn Evening in the Provinces

All the waste land grows wild and tangled
at the town's edge, the papers and tin cans
blowing, rolling on a sudden autumn wind
coming in over the downs from the coast,
with the clouds forming and reforming, blue
and grey and white, reflected in shop windows,
and the church clock slow as it always is.

The shoppers have gone home, the children
have stopped running with their arms
outstretched, the jumble sales are over now,
the streets are dead and alive with
the evening coming on, all the contraceptive
machines begin to drop out their packets,
the pub handles are given a last polish,
cinema seats bang down like gunfire.

In the council houses a last touch of powder,
a smoothing down of hair, leaving
the flickering screen for their parents.
The young move towards the town centre,
the discos will be opening soon, the sun
will be gone, the moon will transform
the beer cans. Something else will be transformed,
a life, a shrub near the high rise flats, a hand
gently resting on a willing thigh, the whole
of life, after the clock's slow tick,
the dull day of work and snatched sandwiches,
the gutting of herrings and the factory floor.

They are out for the evening in another world,
which has its own kind of truth and delight,
a kind of wild poetry before the duties
and the babies and the mortgages arrive,
making the downtown trip an impossible dream,
a laugh quavering in the high air.

Cold Turkey

Cold turkey was not a meal to them.
Not that they a made a meal of anything.
Living on social security, their scripts
were food, and hunger was of a different
kind from ours.

Gathered together at the drug centre
they seemed full of life and colour,
as if they had all arrived from some
artists' quarter, in ethnic clothes,
and long hair.

The children played around their feet,
some born addicts, weaned early, placed
in plastic cribs, doing their own
cold turkey, showing withdrawal symptoms,
an hour or so old.

Squatting in vast Regency houses,
they painted the walls with fantasies,
moved out when the police moved in,
leaving their flowers and trees and gods
behind them.

Like nomads they carried their bedding
rolls on their backs, used dirty needles,
bought a little extra heroin on the side,
locked toilets for fixes, quite often
died young like poets.

They cared deeply for each other,
looked out for their friends each week,
were sad when one did not arrive, thought
society owed them a living, went on doubtful
trips to unknown worlds.

Obstinate children, they resisted purification
of any sort, collected snow for the winter
of their discontent, seemed gentle and dreamy
wandering among the hurrying crowds,
towards the sea.

Out of this world, they bore their tribal marks,
bewitched themselves with dope and love,
were agreeable when fed their drugs, but
screamed and shivered when that cold lewd
turkey looked them in the eye.

Opting Out

Shabby, seedy, down-at-heel, they wait
for giro cheques to come, balancing a baby
on one hip, expecting another by a father
they can't quite remember. He was passing
through on an artic to the North and wore
blue jeans, peeled off wads of notes,
had well-rounded buttocks, fucked well.

All children come alike to them. They sit
in the park bawling at the toddlers, feeding
the babies out of plastic bottles. Somehow
they afford yellow hair, but forget to wash
last night's make-up off. Bed-sitters
don't take much cleaning, but like flies,
what happens in the winter weather?

Now, they seem idle and dim in cheesecloth
blouses, an almost idyllic group, making
the hurrying tight-lipped middle-class
mothers appear clean and anxious, returning
to well-decorated houses, placing babies
in hygienic cots, grabbing a quiche quickly
from the freezer. Here, it's fish and chips.

Those children with lustrous brown eyes reveal
the Bangladeshi men who came and went,
leaving their mark behind them. Women
without men seem suddenly to be envied.
Jumble sale and market clothes are easy
to sit around in. Opting out seems OK
from the outside. Inside, what goes on?

Psycho-Geriatric

The social worker comes. She is young with brown arms
and she drives the car with care along the rutted lane.

She bends her head with its springing hair and smiles
with her well-brushed teeth, shifting a little on her chair.

The old woman, whose husband died at Mons, half listens
to all the chat, refuses a hearing aid, eats cold food

straight from the can, hitches her artificial leg on the strap.
The other leg is ulcerated and the yellow pus seeps through.

Somewhere in the East End in 1917 she read the casualty lists
and went away, dry-eyed, to work and keep her two children.

They're doing well. The son has a house in Bognor Regis,
a beer bar and a company car. They visit when they have time.

'My children ask me why I didn't marry a second time.
I say I wouldn't have another man even if he came to me

with a diamond in his arse.' Suddenly we cry with laughter,
her leg squeaks as if it's laughing too. We guess

the social worker has written in her notes 'psycho-geriatric',
but we know better, Hilda and I. We know one day

I'll find her dead, and take away that heavy leg,
and lay her light as a child on her crumpled bed.

999 Call

He lay on the floor covered in shit,
as he had done all night on his fitted carpet.
It could have been a prison cell or torture room,
but it was in fact the biggest flat in town

as he often boasted, pointing out the Bristol glass,
the original prince of Denmark Hill, brought low.

Stepping round the bed I put my foot in it
(as the ambulance men said). Kind men, they kept
the joke to themselves, and the policemen said
they'd be independent too (no bloody geriatric ward
for them). I reported how I'd heard him calling me,
the first Sunday visitor checking on people like him.

As he was driven away, the usual voyeurs drifting
off, he said he didn't want to go, and I took off
my soiled sandals and my tights and washed my feet
in his classy bidet, but although I admired
their way of saying 'You've had some trouble
with your motions, sir', I threw my sandals away.

I threw them away as if they had been him, and yet,
he was an arrogant man the neighbours said,
who once sent hats to Buck House and Ascot, in his time
(those festive hats, those aristocratic faces).
I felt I'd done him dirt, poor chap, and look up
at his louvred windows late at night hoping to see a banner
ELIZABETH, I FORGIVE YOU. NOT YOUR FAULT.
I look, but it is never there.

Night Duty

Float like dead fishes, thoughts do,
Hang like dead chickens, days do.
Drip, drip, the blood from a day's beak,
Limp the brown feathers, unlaid the eggs,
Waiting for the mist to clear and the dogs
To bite and worry the corpse, the sheep
To knit their own wool into fleecy coats
Against the coming, waiting cold.
Crucify and crucify and put him up again,
For the world likes a double death,
Or a double act, especially on a holiday.

I hear death approaching all the time;
Davvy, with the valve in his head,
Henry, dead in two days to shock
And surprise us. Come with your radiotherapy,
Come with your gowns and masks.
Cancerous the days pass and pass,
Night, day, day, night; the wards
Have tragedy polished off the floors
Each morning. Despatch is the thing,
Change the sheets, notify relatives.
Good Morning, Mr Death, I saw you
Last night from the doorway of the sluice,
Carrying a disembowelled chicken for Christmas
On the trolley to the mortuary.
Yes, I saw you as you parted
The swing doors, whistling a tune
Through the gap in your teeth.

The light was not good, but I saw you,
Looking a little fatter, I thought,
A few feathers on your sleeve, some nails
In your pocket perhaps, but certainly
A sound like bone or metal
As the sun came up.

The Intruder

I grow in the dark from nothing.
At first you don't know I am there,
or mistake me, with a frisson of fear,
for my brother, the seeding one.

I grow for no reason, attaching myself
to whichever organs I care to choose,
for until they cut me I have nothing to lose,
and my beauty is never seen.

I grow at my own whim or fancy,
perhaps after you've fallen in the snow,
or later in the season on the patio,
slipping on wet stones after summer rain.

64

I grow to the size only I decide;
an acorn or an apple, secreting
a brown liquid like a greetings
present of soft-centred milk chocolate.

I grow for the hands of the surgeon,
my only admirer, who dangles me before
the camera, catching my profile, whore
that I am, with my insidious ways.

I grow as a child grows and I am rare,
but I am not loved for my fibrous skin,
and after my portrait I am thrown in a bin
to shrivel with all the other intruders.

Red Cell Precursors

In *Figure 1* the carcinoma cells in the bone marrow
look like the abstract paintings found hanging on the walls
of Hampstead houses. Histological section of the marrow
may occasionally reveal tubercles. Painted by Gaucher,
owners may proudly say, but the crowding clumps of cells
are malignant, and not decorative as they suppose.

As you progress further up the softly carpeted stairway
Figure 2 comes as a striking contrast. The bone marrow
is now showing ring sideroblasts, indigo-blue stained
granules round the nuclei of red cell precursors.
The careful arrangement of the rings is masterly,
the colours catch the eye in no uncertain manner.

Figure 3 is the most complex painting of them all.
The trephine biopsy from a patient with aplastic anaemia
shows cellular marrow largely replaced by areas of fat,
meandering cracks like a dried-up reservoir and mapped
Y forks, with cul-de-sacs painted in a delicate shade
of pink, an internal landscape of the body's master.

The owners of these paintings are highly intelligent
educated people, listening intently to the *Art of Fugue*,
drinking wine from their cool cellar as they smoke
cigars, or water the climbing plants in their rooms.
The fact that they tire easily doesn't really worry them
too much. Spotlights fall on *Figures 1* and *2* and *3*.

Government Health Warning

Falling apart at the seams, like a cheap skirt,
I walk round to the off-licence, treading small
Africas of pools after the rain, spying
on lit rooms at people playing happy families
for lonely walkers like me. In the rag trade
they'd class me as a second. I don't keep
up appearances the way I should. A perm
would improve things a lot, my hair,
my thick hair grown slack, like the rest of me.

Clutching my cancer sticks, I feel some pride
the gin doesn't tempt me, makes me sick in fact.
You won't find bottles in my dustbin, sir,
only tins of dog food which I feed my cats.
Perhaps they think they're dogs, retrieving
scraps of lousy poems from the waste basket,
growling when strangers come up the path,
padding uneasily, shoulder to shoulder,
to look like a herd, from room to room.
You might say they don't care the lady's fit
for nothing, doesn't even pleasure a man
these days. I pleasure them, make no mistake,
as one drapes himself like a feather boa
round my neck, the other clawing my tights.

Something is very wrong here. Turning
the corner I see their silhouettes at the window,
remembering that once witches kept cats,
having a quick drag before facing

the humans, who notice disintegration
like surveyors size up the cracks
in old buildings. There is no one to collect
my scattered shards, to see the graceful jar
I once was, before the barbarians moved in,
and the animals circled round, waiting for scraps
of food, or warmth, edging their way into
the group, before things fell apart,
and the rot set in.

Shagged out, I lie down in my cave,
drawing the skins around me. The hunter
has a new wife now, the off-licence lights
are dimmed, a hand turns the notice
to CLOSED, the soft paws creep nearer,
the smoke lingers, not from burning bodies,
but from cigarettes that shorten life.

Inner City Areas

He say he don't know where he's at.
He say it can't go on like this.
He say it turning night into day.
I say baba can't help it, baba
gotta cry. She cry and cry.
I say to get a pail, the roof
leaking again. I say hurry,
but he don't look at me,
or get up, or do nothing.
He just lay on his back
and roll a fag
with his flies undone.

I say I got no money left,
and he turn on me and say,
that kid, that noise, it drive
me up the wall. I tell him no,
don't hurt baba, but he get her

by her little arm and bang her head
on cot. I quiet and baba lay
like doll. I say I gotta get to cas.,
quick like. He say he don't know
how come this happened. Doc say
this too. He sit on chair
and look at me. I don't say nothing.

Lady come next day. She say baba fine
in hospital, but I think they know,
and take her away. When she gone,
before the kids do her car, I say
I think I've fell again,
and all he say is bloody hell.
I say it take two to do it,
and I miss baba even though
she cry and make him bad.

It quiet now, the rain have gone.
We lay down with the tranny on.
The man sing lovely songs
and it get dark. He kiss me
and say he sorry, but he lay
in my arms and cry and cry.

Quite a Day

You didn't say you liked my house.
You just sat down, asking questions,
legs crossed at the ankles, removing
the toddler's hands from your clip-board.
I had washed the coloured crayon marks
off the walls for you, and scrubbed
the rush matting so it smelled as sweet
as summertime in far away Norfolk,
and herded the cats into the garden
so they shouldn't tear your tights.

Cohabiting, you said, as if it was
a gob-stopper stuck in your throat.
The baby sat in the cats' basket
and chewed on a piece of paper
looking gormless. The whole house
looked gormless and done for and shabby,
so very market stall, so very Co-op.
I even felt ashamed of Vermeer's
poor lace-maker, eternally bent over
her work with her high forehead under
the braided and parted hair.

I see, you said, you have a typewriter.
Like owning a rattle-snake, you made it seem.
Do I cohabit with the typewriter?
Do I cook the cats when the allowance is gone?
Do I, hell, do I? No, the children's father
has not married me. Studying for a degree,
you said, and twitched your skirt over
your virginal bottom as you pranced through
the hall and over the grubby Oxfam mat,
neatly dressed with your navy-blue hat.

'Go way,' shouted the toddler, 'go way.'
His first linked words. It was quite a day.

Multiple Fractures

The first a greenstick fracture
in a gas-lit bedroom saying no,
let me go, her Jew's nose
already too large for a small
child screaming.

The second a hair-line
no orthopaedic consultant saw,
saying no, let me go,
I won't, but fists had no strength,
his were hard.

Then, multiple fractures,
a cracked heart saying no,
I can't, cuckooing in and out
of psychiatric wards,
a baby crying.

Finally, the spine gave way,
her daughter dead on the road,
a funeral, saying no, I can't go,
face in a crooked mirror,
crumpled like a rag.

Charlotte, Her Book

I am Charlotte. I don't say hello
to people and sometimes I bite.
Although I am dead I still jump
out of bed and wake them up at night.

This is my mother. Her hair is blue
and I have drawn her with no eyes
and arms like twigs. I don't do
what I'm told and I tell lies.

This is my father. He has a mouth
under his left ear. I'm fed up
with drawing people, so I scribble
smoke and cover his head right up.

I am a brat kid, fostered out because
my mother is sick in the head,
and I would eat her if I could,
and make her good and dead.

Although I am only four I went away
so soon they hardly knew me,
and stars sprang out of my eyes,
and cold winds blew me.

My mother always says she loves me.
My father says he loves me too.
I love Charlotte. A car ran
over Charlotte. This is her book.

Sasha's Room

(a translation from childhood)

Sasha's room is filled with books.
It is so small there's no space
for a wardrobe, his crumpled clothes
lie on a chair, hang on hooks.

Sasha's room is full of apples,
laid out on the bed, a body
of apples laid out from pillow
to foot with red dreamers' faces.

He wasted his substance away here
in a white room like a prison cell,
a wooden chair, a bed, a sketch
of bulls to catch the sun's day.

His fantasies hit the walls,
his night sweats and hot terrors
ripen like fruit in his absence,
his shivering voice rises and falls.

He thought this town should be
razed to the ground, the ugly church,
the park, the children's cement pool.
I was your room once. You laid in me.

Sasha's room is full of Sasha now.
He drove off to Moscow, somewhere
to find himself, where people talk
and ride in troikas on new snow.

Come, little Sasha, put your shoes
under the bed. I know how hard it is
to leave this compartment of life,
for what you have you always lose.

Alexander, or more familiarly, Sasha,
your beard needs trimming neatly,
your shabby clothes mark you out,
your shining hair smells of apples.

Someone came out of Sasha's room
just now, although the door was shut.
I am sorry my translation is so bad,
but a small dictionary was all I had.

Tripos

He sleeps with his B.A. under his belt at last,
but flat, after exam euphoria, his First seeming
somehow, to be nothing, after appearing to be
everything.

You sleep, too, beside me, trying to get the accounts
right, or dreaming Big School has been shifted, that
hallowed and not so ancient pile, to a Nissen hut,
and the corporal on guard has unexpectedly fainted
in the snow, and the rations have not yet come.

The cats sleep, re-living the day one caught
a budgie, the blue feathers floating round
the garden. He hopped tamely to them, crying
pretty boy, and their claws reduced him
fairly soon to a mangled pile of red entrails,
and a small hooked beak, not edible.

I lay awake, whose habitat is bed, thinking
of the graceful spring and the stabbing wound,
remembering the celebration of an honours degree,

coldly laying the guests bare, stripping
their masks, their fears showing like ribs,
the spite just underneath the bonhomie,
the pulse beating in the swallowing throat,
the irresolute stomach churning beneath
the ethnic dresses and the trendy suits.

I wonder if I should have picked away at the flesh
like that, reducing my pretty boys to a pile
of half-eaten food, their lives to feathers,
moving in the slight wind which is getting up,
and blowing the curtains, thumbing through
the Tripos papers, reviving the fallen corporal,
frisking over graves and cages and empty
college quadrangles and pedestrian precincts.

A poem knocks and throbs like a bird in my head,
bigger than a budgie, smaller than an osprey
neither familiar nor rare, just there, waiting
for the sleepers to wake, and the nest to reveal
its broken shells. Someone has been bird-nesting.
The eggs lie yolk-spattered, useless
as a question on tragedy, or an account ruled off,
unresolved. Big School topples brick by brick.

Contre Jour

Contre jour, he said, a photographic phrase,
literally against the day, I suppose.
I'll put a little by, my mother would say,
against the day when we have nothing left.
Limp purse, well-rubbed, false teeth
not quite fitting, second-hand clothes,
knees like nutmeg graters. Whatever happened
to those gentle scented mothers sitting in gardens
under a shady hat, the maid mincing across the grass
with a tray for afternoon tea in early June?
It was never summer for her. It didn't reach

the dank back yard, the airless little rooms,
where the kitchen range brought a flush
to her face as she perpetually bent over it,
cooking, ironing, shifting sooty kettles round,
but never posed for her husband to catch
the tilt of her head against the day,
who never owned a camera anyway.

My inner lens clicks faster, faster,
contre jour, for now her face is fading
as her life recedes. You must have known
that once she minced across the lawn
carrying a loaded tray for mothers
like yours, whose photographs have
frames of silver, like the ones
she polished every week for twelve
pounds per annum and her keep.

Second Wife

Someone has been here before me.
The trap was sprung and out ran
a silver fox from the suffocating box,
leaving her litter of two behind her.
Substitute a young brown mouse
and close the trap again for the hunter
to find, his bold one gone over the hills
to Wales, and this startled creature
huddled in a corner to be taken home
in his big warm hands, reared to come
for food, obedient to his call.

She wore black underwear, I know,
from scraps of knowledge garnered
from wheat ears left lying in the stubble,
middle-class, with a yen for the stage,
The wedding took place in the spring
in a Wesleyan chapel. How much notice

did they take of the paintings
in the Louvre, I wonder, fox to hunter,
aspiring writer to solicitor's daughter,
the honeymoon paid for by her father?
They couldn't have heard dictator's speeches.

They couldn't have heard the quiet sounds
mice make behind Parisian walls, squeaking
in perfect French. Some few came before me,
the litter have had their young in their turn,
the bright brand of the fox dominant over
all the genes, returning like new growth
over fields of burnt out flax, where
predator and prey struggle for survival.
Fox, fox, hear me. I will reverse the laws
of nature and see you cower under
my feeble paw, my sparkling flying one.

Unrequited Love

Salivating like Pavlov's dogs, I respond to signals
of distress, not food, put on my clinical hat,
offer you anti-depressants for a wound too deep
for chemistry to touch, and try in vain to find you.

I have to accept that you will always be just
out of reach, that to lie between paper sheets
is the nearest we shall ever get to love. Turn
a computer cross just slightly, and it makes a kiss.

In the end, as they say, words seem to fail me,
and putting on my poet's hat I could wish it was
the plastic bag which now is the ultra-modern way
out of all the stanzas of free-fall delusion.

I never thought my bitch's drooling mouth
would be so eager for the meal that never came,
that you would be my white-coated master,
calling me to heel, wearing your laboratory hat.

These animals, they copulate so rapidly.
Perhaps we should have done the same,
a forceful thrust against the railings
of the hospital, but, no, that's not the way.

You never liked my colloquial way with words.
I mock the only gods I ever had this way,
knowing that they are all I really cared for,
and all the rest is just a tale of unrequited love.

Yesterday's Face

Evening is walking in the white tiled caverns of the subway,
is like pacing through palaces and pleasure gardens.
Someone has washed away the grey faces and lit
the incense sticks, the blowing papers are pale leaves
tangled round my ankles, and I descend into the pit
with sacrificial gestures. For a day the world went away.

Night is like the laying down of burdens which school prayers
promised. I know the meaning of peace and I feel
it like a confirmation veil over my head and on my thighs.
Fingers rest in secret pools and in sleepy silence,
like they always said, the scales fall from my eyes,
the sick rise up, the child is alive like a warm dove.

Morning is sunlight and waking in the wrong bed,
my arm stretched out to roll away that heavy stone.
My Lord is risen and the coffee is waiting there,
but the dreams are draining away, the songs of praise
turn into the plainsong of reality, combing hair,
washing away yesterday's face, stamping on hymnals.

Visions are for saints. There's no holy light here.
The soft wafers on the tongue turn into daily bread.
The Fire went out. If there's a god he's gone
on a walk-about, the laying on of hands today
is scheduled for the District Line, passengers fall upon
their knees, the ten commandments are written on the wall.

It was yesterday's face which broke them all.

To His Dry Mistress

I need this drink to get through the day.
The hour gets earlier each day, each week,
each month. There is more to celebrate,
less to care about, more quarrels, misty
lost days, lost lives; whisky colours
everything. In a whisky velvet suit,
my love comes asking for her small glass
of water, but I laugh and throw it
in her face. She is the one I found
too late, and tried to share my life
and poems with. She is a pure white
lady with a small bottom and a dead tooth,
to whom I never dared to tell the truth,
carrying her keys with spectral gravity.

I am the one that barmen know,
and my wife knows me too. The smell
of my breath is not like honey and roses,
and the smell of my death doesn't please
her. That I drown daily gives sorrow
its name. From alpha to gamma
to beta, I saw my straight-fringed
one who drank half a glass of wine,
a sherry, and I thought her mine,
until the epsilon was staged in front
of her, and she broke all the glasses
in the fireplace of my drunken love.

End of a Marriage

He was afraid she might board a train to a place
where they had been happy and take her own life.

She was also afraid she might do that very thing.
It had occurred to her so often as she woke in despair

each morning, waiting for the dead world to show
some colour, and the sweating terror to ease a little,

facing the nadir of the day, naked as a fledgling
tipped out of the nest into a world of predators.

He was a lover of life, walking the uplands in sun
or rain, a rational man, finding joy in small things,

his skin was weathered, and his stride was long
and purposeful, his voice deliberate and measured.

She, on the other hand, always looked ill, even on
her better days. She slept a lot, and walked very little,

cried for no reason, and was as hopeless in argument
as she was at living in the real world at all.

That they were both afraid was a mystery to them,
and so the marriage died, but no one noticed this.

He was naturally thought by everyone to be the nicer
of the two. Health and joy and love of the world appealed.

She appeared to them by contrast a poor thing,
grudging, sallow and unfriendly. Her skilfully executed

paintings confounded them all. His pompous memoirs
dismayed his admirers. They felt that life had somehow

let them down. She should have been the untalented one,
and he should have been the giver of life, the genius.

Guitars as Women

Guitars as women, men hold them
on their laps, decorated with
mother-of-pearl and ivory,
necklace them with patterns

of sound, run fingers up and down,
play them tenderly with their fingers,
play them fiercely with plectrums,
knocking on wood.

Laid in green baize or leaning
against walls, they wait,
guitars, like women for orgasms
of chords, hand flat on the strings,
the notes stopped like a cry.

Headless, but scrolled, each one
different, flamenco or transcribed
lute music, they shiver down the frets,
their *haute couture* of ribbons
tremble, sound bleeds out,
their bellies have a high sheen,
their waists are gut-strung.
Women as guitars.

Saint-Severin

Walking into pictures, some of us perch
on the haywain, like a TV ad, happy
to be in a world of trees and sweet smells,
and maybe somewhere young women waiting.

It would be difficult to walk into Picasso,
avoiding the one-eyed people and the bulls,
escaping the swift cloak with one leap,
waiting in vain for a note from the blue guitar.

All the tired business men might creep
into the massive bosoms of Rubens' ladies
and lie curled there, bedded down
until the next dull board-room meeting.

I walk up Utrillo's street. Only a few people
pass idly by on the pavement, the balconies
are neatly arranged on the first white building.
A pity Saint-Severin is locked, but no matter.

It is quiet, and the trembling branches pattern
the walls, the ornate lamp-post fits well
into the hollow of my back as I wait
for the restaurant to open, to take some wine.

Walking into pictures, it is hard to return
without hay on a cuff, the beast's smell,
powder on the paunchy suit, the imprint
of a wine-glass stem, backwards into today.

An Answer to Blake

He had been doing it for years;
a kindly man, his skill was admirable.
First he picked up the dead lamb,
and then he competently skinned it,
leaving the head, like a puppet,
hanging on the outhouse door, the hooves
and entrails somehow out of place
dangling below the toy-shop face.
Then he cut four small holes
in exactly the right places,
and fitted this little bloody coat
on the live lamb, leaving him to trot
to the ewe who was not his mother,
but sniffed the false fleece
and, puzzled, allowed him to suckle.
Something is not quite right,
her foolish face seemed to say,
but the smell is of my flesh
for which I am bred and therefore
must accept. Outside the snow
falls. There will be other lambs
born dead tonight, and coats to make.

Mistaken Identity

Dear Miss Barrett, we would like to include two of your
poems in an anthology of satirical and abusive verse.
                                        PUBLISHER'S LETTER

Although it's true my name is Elizabeth,
I don't have ringlets, and a quick cut
and blow-dry is all I can manage these days.
I was named after my grandmother's mother
who was taken away to an asylum after years
in a coastguard station with only the sea
for company and rough weather in her marriage.

Although it is true I write poems of a sort
and often in bed, this is mostly because the rest
of the furniture is uncomfortable or the television
is on showing another Elizabeth catching sight
of the shrunken heads on poles, the royal barge
bumping against the steps of the Tower,
her orange hair plastered to her skull.

I don't have a Mr Browning to smuggle me
away, make me pregnant and boldly set me
on my feet. The most I can run to is a man
who stalks wild deer and hills and clouds
with a zoom lens and a fragile light-meter
and the curious habit of writing a journal,
recording weather, villages, footpaths, people.

I don't have a lapdog, but lap cats, who curl
on either side of me for warmth. Sometimes
I wake thinking I am paralysed. It is only
the soft bodies numbing my legs, and hardly
psychosomatic. I have to admit the name Flush
doesn't really appeal, any more than walkies
and leads and bald patches on the lawn.

All in all, the mistake is an unfortunate one,
although I think maybe her Papa was very like
mine, dictatorial, humourless and with incest
not so very far away. I have to be thankful
he didn't bring me porter in a glass.

I never saw a house in Wimpole Street,
just a two-up and two-down in a seaside town.

I don't really mind. The launching of the book
was most interesting. Wedged between Winnie
(the Pooh), and the Authorised Version I kept
a watchful eye on a fellow poet with a
Gucci bag in case I had to lead him home,
and as most of the contributors were dead,
a good time was had by all who were alive.

Goodbye, Dan Defoe

I crept up Grub Street, three quarters stoned
with gin.
On a quiet night, and there weren't many,
I heard
the sounds of Bedlam, and I knew the rats
by name.
Goodbye, Dan Defoe. Nice to have met you,
even in the company of an M.A. Ph.D.,
numb-arsed, and learning fast.
It was fashionable to have a French sounding name,
so you ranted against it.
The next we knew, Lord help us,
you were Dan Defoe, or Daniel
in the centuries to come, for all
true born Englishmen.
We went to the stinking open sewer
called London,
under the very kind auspices of the University,
picking our way
past the dung heaps where the unwanted babies
nestled in the warm to die.
Yes, they were the good old days,
when you could pin a sailor to a wall
by his ear,
or drop a howling cat from a height,

for a bit of a giggle,
or even rape a twelve year old,
with the blood warm from a cock-fight
still on your hands.
Blood to blood, ashes to ashes,
worm to worm, in Bunhill Fields.
Indefatigable Foe, who died
of a lethargy,
would you believe?
and shoved us all on the road to the great
English novel,
via the pillory and the old Review.
You meet us here at lectures,
you shifty old opportunist,
so here's to you, Honest Dan,
I see you're still around.

The Moscow Metro

My fur hat was slipping, and as I said
to Sergei, these platforms are too wide:
Whatever would they go and do a thing
like that for? He didn't say anything.
His fur hat was a good fit. A man
doesn't worry about a thing like that –
always talking about bombs and war
and dual-purpose subways. Up in the air,
the snow stinging our cheeks, he looked back
to the wide underground spaces with a stare
like a death mask, and we went home together,
Sergei and I, and I began to wonder again
if he really noticed my hat in the subway train.

Front Door

*There is no teachable technical skill in writing, despite
the courses in American colleges; to become a writer is
not like becoming a physician, ballet dancer, or trombonist.
There is no academic degree that a poet or novelist can
polish on his front door.*

ANTHONY BURGESS

With two thirds of the population writing verse,
or what we in the trade call poetry, or worse,
what would we be doing with a rag and a tin
of brass polish shining up that too-soon dulled
metal, ineptly screwed on doors with flaking paint?

Trained like dancers to perform amazing feats,
practising daily at our home-made barre, no one greets
our efforts with a carefully thrown red rose,
a doxology or compliment, and trombone players
save their breath for much more taxing work.

As for physicians, they are too busy looking down throats,
up vaginas, into bloodshot eyes, deciphering their own notes
to bother about the ones who labour on, using tools
like pararhymes, instruments of feeling, medicines
to purge the soul, tapping out words on worn-out keys.

Picking verbal scabs we're not the kind you'd hope
to find arranged around your dining table, or drop
in for a game of Scrabble, Lexicon or cards.
We have no useful academic honours, which means
you've dropped yourself right in it for a start.

We don't deserve perhaps to use this form of art.
A poem should be full of tender phrases, part
of a long and noble tradition, or describe landscapes
where the rocks and stones seem almost photographic.
You could write as well as me. Paper is all you need.

Chapter Headings

What has happened when the face doesn't fit
the feelings any more? The body stays
much as it was, flat stomach, sloping shoulders,
hair coarse and thick, but not long, not now.
But the face: it shows how many tears
and tempers and disappointments erode the skin
like sea washing on crumbling coastlines.

It begins with the first frown of concentration
over an exam paper, and the need to come top.
Lines score deeper after endless broken nights,
and the 2 a.m. feed, monstrous whizz kid,
a line of washing, the double-think of double beds,
fix on it the look which searched the shallow hole,
a small death, but a cosmetic disaster, like
a kind of endless chapter heading to a novel
which will close one day, remaindered.

Eunuch Death, who will review, will say
the last third of the book was filled
with soft arms and lips, sly sessions
in station photobooths, trying to gain
an illegal passport back to youth,
but unstamped, no longer able to travel
the world as female conqueror.

He will say it could all have been cut
severely, but I don't agree with this.
Face as mirror, life as instalments –
it's so corny. Reader, don't go on.
Your heroine is doing it all in reverse,
her ravaged face doesn't fit her feelings.
She is just a naughty child dancing behind the hearse,
pulling her eyes down and her mouth up, a gargoyle
spouting rain from futile filling gutters, while
the stiff wired flowers brown and wither and spoil.

A Plea for Mercy

For all the poor little sods who shoot themselves off
in boarding schools and dormitories, jerking into sleep,

and all the prissy girls who ride their horses bareback
or wet their knickers and seats at noisy pop concerts,

there are always the others who will, in the end, read
Divinity, or spend the rest of their life praying

to that pregnant girl, or join the prison service,
clamping an eye to the hole in the locked cell door.

In mental hospitals the patients masturbate quite openly,
with dreamy spiritual faraway faces, not much to lose,

and knowing they are listed for the high jump next day
anyway, passing the uneven hours between doctor's rounds

and basket making. If they go blind, well, they should care.
In the penumbra of their distorted world so many shadows,

and such fragile transparent pleasures. From dormitories
to geriatric homes and all the institutions in between,

a fair fantasy, a brief respite, and a dreamless sleep,
before the matrons, doctors, screws and curates muscle in.

Salad Dreams

I am like the lady who dreamed
she prepared a salad for her guests
and grated her own skin over it.
Women and food, eating for two,
the procreator, the sick mornings,
the recurring nightmare of banquets
and not enough to go round.

If we could get away from the noise
of consciousness, we might dream
all day, exhorting, frightening,
talking to ourselves. The pathology
of poetry is like the life we lead
at night, in which we freely bleed,
fly without wires, scream without sound.

Pushing at bulging frontiers with hands
too weak to understand, we do not
write for our audiences, but to convince
ourselves of our own reality, and since
we reach a little further down
than most, words are like probes,
and salads are prepared with care.

An involuntary kind of poetry, we fail
to interpret the messages which push up
in dreams, destroy their innocence
with defiant acts and masochistic knives,
turning our loving friends away
at the door, living like frugal hermits
on lettuce leaves and grated skin.

A Pastoral Crime

Your face is slowly going out of focus, blurring
at the edges, indistinct. The mountain is the man,
the man is staring out across unknown distances
of time and space. I think I see a brutal murder
being committed, but no, it was only the hymen
torn too quickly, the blood was on my thigh:
the membrane of a closed mind was split as well.

A commonplace act, no worse than a cut finger;
I have no cues for melodrama, and the villain
wondered what all the fuss was about, as you
do now, appearing to be alone, but photographed

88

by an unknown hand which held the camera still,
as if quite sure that there would be no cause
for frantic running over leaves and bracken.

That I have one skin too few is not news to you.
I could pull one on and fake it, but you would
soon pull off my protective covering and repeat
that pastoral crime and not repent the deed, for
no one would ever lay it at your door or blame you
for so natural and everyday an act. She must have
led him on, they'd say, and laugh, as you do now.

The few drops of blood dried quickly, the ferns
sprang up, uncurled, and only the wood anemone
was crushed and brown under the drumming heels.
Up on the downs they lead the horses out, to trot,
and then to gallop into the biting wind, manes
flying, tails lifted, the stallions and the mares,
blinkered and urged forward to win the race.

Mademoiselle Miss

Cherche-Midi, and Tiger sharpening her claws
on the wicker chair; Burgess Hill and Bathsheba
doing the same. After all the solitary years,
wicker is in again, perhaps because times
are hard and creaking whispering chairs
are cheap and durable, made by deft hands
in Taiwan.

She stood by the window, in her nightdress, listened
to the nightingale. I only hear Hondas with their
monstrous purr, revving up, and screams in the dark.
She had no carpets and no ornaments, just a bunch
of primroses on a wooden table, and Rodin's gift,
that precious wardrobe, a lover's closet, a secret
hiding place.

Like me, she changed her few possessions round,
the damp green fern, the mat, and painted the tiles
on the floor rose-red, sat in the sun like the small
fur-bearing animals she loved, endured her flu
each year, feeding only her cats, growing thin
in her own third world, laughed about the flasher
on the stairs.

A vest drying over a chair, perhaps newly washed
after the Sunday sessions behind thc screen;
a half-finished painting: 'I'm not going to cry,'
she wrote, 'I am going to buy two eggs.'
Anorexic, she wore her cerise faille for him.
I wear my green, stand in draughty halls
to see you pass.

Mademoiselle Miss: The name given to Gwen John by the
concierge's husband who used to expose himself on the stairs.

Man, Eating Apples

The smell of wrinkled apples fills the house.
In October I ate them greedily, now I chew
on them, ashamed to buy correctly stored Cox's
from supermarkets. They are like the mistresses
I had, the firm fruit fresh from the tree,
now just past middle age, frowning slightly
without their glasses, lined and over-ripe.

The one I spent a brief two days with is dead.
It was war-time and she lay under me quietly
like a doll. 'Thanks for a super weekend,'
she said on the station platform. One has gone
back to Europe, cherishes her nephews, young Jews,
cultured and fastidious as she was. She washed
after love with chilling haste. Do they?

Girls in uniform in army camps, now all late
soft apples, the juices dried up, the skin
of their breasts loose and their hair fading
from brown to white, as mine is, now, as well.
Lovely, then, the bloom and the small curve
of their bellies, the sweet juice still fresh
as I drank in the arrogance of my prime.

My wife shuts the bedroom door and sleeps
with her arm over her eyes. She was the diseased
globe on the lowest branch of the tree,
attacked by her illness like a codlin moth,
yet her angular body was far more tempting
in its youthful virginity than the cider apples
crushed in heavy presses, stored in barrels.

I drank her nineteen years with a thirsty greed
which I have never had since then, raped her orchard
and pruned her tender branches with my knife
and saw her rot in waking nightmares daily.
Eating apples, I look back and wonder if
I should have left her to fall to the earth
and not gone scrumping like a careless boy.

Therefore My Grandmother in Sepia

In colour films, the past is shown
in black and white, the very distant
past in sepia.

Therefore my grandmother in sepia,
although actually in a black and white
apron, sits in our back yard,
her stage-set a lattice of ivy leaves
grown to hide the outdoor privy.
A widow, since women even then
were survivors, her dead babies
lay in little boxes, quiet children,

as you might expect them to be.
I bore ten and reared three,
she used to say to me.

I read the whole of *Jane Eyre*
to her, the Woolworths glasses
she wore being useless and the print
too small. Together we were shut
into the red room, and heard
the laughter in the upper rooms.
Mr Rochester was her lover,
as well as mine, but she
would never admit it.

She sits, the proud husk from which
we came, keeping her Armistice Day
poppy from one year to the next,
coloured blood red, then black and white,
and fading into sepia,
like her babies' father, who marched
jerkily away at the wrong speed,
appearing to hurry eagerly to war,
because of a technique which is faulty,
but which, with care, may be altered,
although the perpetual blizzard may not.

Waiting Room

In charge of the surgery waiting room
I now wait myself to hear news of illness.
I am the one dreading renal failure, a coronary.
Your pain is mine. Let me take it from you.
To stand by and watch, the patients said,
is always the worst part. Yes, I said, yes,
thinking of letters arriving, poems to write,
new clothes, growing my hair to just that length
which might please you, having felt your hand
twisting that short crop I had a few months ago.

Not in charge of my emotions, I have already
lost you to the surgeon's knife. That you
abused your body to keep going, I knew already,
but did not think the daily trivia I use
would mock me as I filled in forms for X-rays,
wrote scrips for killing pain and easily
asked if there was any blood, any vomiting.
Picking my hangnail idly, I listened in to voices
describing symptoms which I clearly wrote,
tuning in to a personal message of hope and dread.

Mediator between doctor and patient, you said.
If I could be your go-between, I would doctor
all those other ills you have, and you would know
the waiting room I've been living in for news
of you which doesn't come. I am the one
who must not accompany you or send flowers,
and all those crazy get-well tokens which
clutter up lockers as if a birthday had come,
instead of love, which came too late and was denied,
turned away by pickets holding official union cards.

Voyeur

Watching from the bed, with a bleeding cunt
and gin-painted nipples, she saw at last
what he meant about having had a certain
nobility in his youth. Outside, the vast
sky met the grey sea, and the white pier
broke in half, falling in slow motion.
For days the beach looked like an antique
fair, and children travelled to the ocean
to peer through Victorian iron scrolls.

Watching from the road, with her tart's kit
hidden in a plastic bag, she spied him
watering the flowers on his balcony – a tit
and bum man with a fatal heart disease,

a penchant for dirty books and prayer,
an actor's way of playing to the gallery,
but, sitting at his mirror, removing layers
of make-up, when the act was over.

Watching from the chair, he saw her arm
rise from the crumpled sheets, waving
or beckoning, and wished he was shocked
by her pallor, and heard her wild raving
about a pier, some child or other, crying
'I'm sorry' as if she had knocked
it down with her fist. Caged in iron,
she woke to find his eyes staring.

Watching from the bed, he saw his young mother
loosen her stays and lean forward to
peel off her garters and stockings. Feigning sleep
as she slid in beside him, he half knew
that somewhere there would be a great sea,
a pier falling, a woman with frail bones
and big breasts, nameless, faceless, who
would suck on him like waves suck stones,
and he would be a man, waiting, watching.

Lyke-Wake

It sounds like a folk song.
At £1 an hour it is not so much
a folk song as a trial,
a Weltschmerz, a lachrimae rerum.
To be privileged and paid by the council
is not like a song, and the doctor
doesn't wish to be called until morning
with sliding notes and semi-quavers
as he lies by his wife for his own
few hours of oblivion.

If death occurs early in the evening,
as the pubs open and the lights come on,

the ballad is accepted, if with a bad grace,
but just before dawn, wait a bit,
and keep the lyke-wake, clear up
the last liquids which issue from
all the orifices except the ears.
There is always a moment when the music
stops. Can he hear me?
he can see me, but can he hear?

I have to sing the last chorus alone.
It is so quiet I am almost happy
in the Victorian role of sitter-in.
The money buys me poems
from hand presses, records
of folk songs.
Would you care for my services any time?
I am skilled at closing eyes
and singing grace notes,
as well as changing sheets.

A Good Old Bed

She showed me where the poet
had laid down his austere head,
and fitted on to his shape,
his foam of words flooding
her cavity wall of pelvic bone,
his thoughts slicing into her crisp
cauliflower of brain, his rhythms
variously pulsing round her blood.

All night his sea-birds called
through her dreams and pewter seas
darkened her hair from light brown
to black, frilling round her ankles
and pouring out of her eyes,
salt tears licked with a tongue
too quick to scold and swallowed
like atonement or warm blood.

It was a good old bed, well-made
and comfortable, she said, clutching
a hot water bottle. If she'd had him
she wouldn't have needed it, but he
was flying high, climbing podiums,
crossing the Atlantic, coast-to-coasting,
warming up some other cold woman
with his soft skin and hot blood.

'Now I lay me down to rest' and
rigid as a statue on a regal tomb
she watched the moon's last quarter.
Sun rises at eight, and she gets up
from habit, slides into trousers
and blouse, sets her heart in place
and covers up the stains. Sun's up,
and so is the anger in her blood.

Drop dead, drop dead. I never wanted this.
A good old bed.

Deviant

I know you. I saw you once following me
along the tow path by the canal. A bicycle
reared rusty handle-bars from the grey water,
and your grubby mac flapped round your knees.
I only waited for the first button to be undone,
and ran instinctively, scraping my knuckles
on walls and wire, back to the milling people
and the fancy hat shops and the staring windows
of arcades which sold no such clothes as the ones
you wore.

I know you. I saw you again at the back
of the bandstand where the paint had hardly dried
from the summer season, creeping past the piles
of municipal deck chairs, stencilled on the backs,
brown canvas piles, folded and unfolded each day,

a screen for your ambush; a knot of string
round your old army coat this time and a hat
from nowhere, palpable and shapeless, mildewed
with age and rain. I went round to the front,
seeing your strange gaze.

I know you, because I was your victim, going
for solitary walks at odd times of the day,
carrying my books and my brown bag of scraps
for stray cats, avoiding the holiday crowds.
You are a victim also, in your own curious way,
loitering in lonely places, patiently waiting
like a bird-man in a shuffling shabby hide,
with your sudden quick and sad revelation
of unattainable memory, picking your girls
with a practised eye.

Toller Fratrum

The Toller Fratrum people,
carved in soft Dorset stone
have held up the font
for nine hundred years
or so.

The mason who fashioned
these dolls out of stone
laughed as he hacked
the last face upside down,
chewed on black bread,
picked up his tools
and stumbled out
into the 11th century.

He has no name, was perhaps
one of many itinerant
fantasy makers,
pissed behind the wall,
and went where?

Along the draughty aisle
they clatter, chattering,
doll-mouths changed
from slits to Os,
skitter back to the font
when visitors come,
play tig around the pews
when they go.

Schizophrenia

If anyone comes, asking if I am here,
tell them I have gone away.

I have gone into no voices for the speaking with,
under gargoyles with ears for all hearing with,
wet with streaked tears for no weeping with,
and cannot come when you call
with your high voices through the wall,
you changing people, grown large, grown small
for my torment.

If a man comes, carrying golden apples,
tell him I will have none.

I have no use for apples not for the eating of,
or a heart rigid for the loving with,
and my stained clothes will never be for the cleaning of.
Your hands lift me up and out of my bed,
your white starch rustle-talks
for my torment.

If a woman comes, holding a child by the hand,
tell her it is not mine.

I have a hollow which is not for the filling of,
and breasts which have no hope for the sucking from,
and a demon who is not for the killing of.

I am alone for the loneliest dream there is dreaming of.
Your drugs are white grit in my mouth,
for my poisoning, for my dying of,
for my torment.

But if a child comes alone with an armful of toys,
tell her I am here in my bed.

Her doll is for my clasping and my talking to,
and her puppets for my playing and my fondling of,
her giants and her dead princesses for my looking at,
her birth for my death, on a sheet for the winding in,
her silence for my psaltery of laughter,
no dirtier and no dafter
than I ever was.

Heart and Soul

Your heart you left in an upstairs room,
lying on the mat, pulsating slowly,
which was careless of you and scared me
half to death.

Your soul you left on the turn of the stairs,
like a giant cobweb. I nearly broke my neck
trying to get it down.

Your body moves off along the Fulham Rd,
taking your mind with it, so no more
clearing up for me to do.
Take them. I should care.

I keep your heart and soul in the cupboard
under the stairs, the heart propped
between the boys' skateboards,
and Ma's old sewing-machine,
your soul pushed well to the back,
it floats so easily, hard to store.

If you should ever leave your mind
behind somewhere, or worse, your body,
I hope their keepers don't get the fright
I had, whether they find you shrugged off
on some bathroom floor, or in a noose
to greet them behind their own front door.

They'd need to collect your gear
from me some time. The cupboard is small
and your heart and soul are uneasy there.
I hear them moving sometimes in the night,
as if they wanted to follow you on the tube,
startling the passengers, and offending
the ticket collector.

Perhaps you'll collect them yourself,
when you are passing.
I wish that I was rid of them,
once and for all,
with all my heart and soul.

Student Demo

He called her a Kraut. Too much
of the old Sieg Heil, he thought,
and yet he married her, a woman
he could not fuck and who liked
her meals dead on time and hot.

He thought he was teaching her
English, but German phrases crept
into his speech as he searched
for lost papers, elastoplast
and a few aspirintabletten.

One cunt is much like another.
How his tongue slid over brutal
words, describing how he bumped
into his first wife's ghost
in the empty flat, at first.

Somehow he had to fill the void,
the quiet carpeted rooms, the bed.
It didn't work out and he was
uptight most of the time, never
laughed and rarely even smiled.

Durfte ich um das salz bitten?
They sit across the table talking
to each other. She is light and neat,
he is heavy with melancholy thoughts,
looking down into the noisy square.

The student demo stirs something
in him. Put your son in the army,
he once said. Nein, Herr Docktor,
he is mine, with his gentle smile
and has no taste for blood or salt.

The banners look like silken scarves
and wars bleed into each other –
Mafeking, Gallipolli, Cassino,
Vietnam, Afghanistan, but the cry
which spirals up is Lebanon.

He was a student once, but only
got a third. Too busy chasing
girls was his excuse. His war
is across the dining table,
far away from demos of today.

With My Body

With your hand, like that, he said.
Somebody's radio played, the quilt
was covered in flowers, the wine glass
had a stem; his stem was unfamiliar.
The sun flew through the room. I said
in bed, so soon? I hardly know you.

101

With your mouth, like that, he said;
a first communion, a milky wine,
a pubic hair on my tongue, a time
to remember. People keep strands
of hair in lockets. I keep this one
like a saint's relic. He was no saint.

With your whole life, like that, he said.
I never had a life, not until now,
and I never knew this curious way before.
I was always taken flat on my back,
but this was feast day after fast,
and still goes on although it's past.

Tresaith
(for Anna Lloyd)

We only lived here for the sound
of a short summer's drag and pull
of the changing tides, the sound
of the Welsh voices under our sill
as different, and as alien to our ears,
as the voices which immigrant Jews
may hear in New York before the echo
of words fades from the high ghetto
walls, and the syllables are blown
by the city winds through the arcade,
the viaduct, the cinema hall.

In this village only the dripping
arcades of the caves, no viaduct,
no cinema, only the single road
rising up and out to Aberporth,
and the gentle archaic voices
surrounding us for the time of day,
and the rain setting in early,
and who saw Evans the Post, and the milk
is late coming down from Dyffrynsaith,
and always, the sound of the sea.

The bracken is trodden along the cliff,
as it was when we were there,
but Anna is dead. The sea-grass is stiff
and coarse where the road ends,
but Anna is dead. The lamps are lit
in the stuffy parlours, and the sea
draws close to the empty summer huts,
washing the sand covered steps; tea
is laid, but not for us, and the hard
little apples drop from the tree
on to the grey stones of the yard.

A place like this is hard to forget,
not only for the brief huddle
of bleached houses, or the feel
of a charred wick in the hand, or a net
and a row of green glass balls
found on an unswept attic floor,
but for the comprehension of the sadness
of a lost race, and for the first
years of a marriage, and an old woman
called Anna Lloyd who opened her rooms
to us, and now is dead and buried.

Not Dead But Sleeping

She didn't lie long, they said,
clutching their soiled dressing gowns
to their wrinkled drooping breasts.
It was a mercy really.

There is a death in the home,
a room is vacant now, her bottles
of gin have been whisked away,
her library books returned.

The Victorian drains smell foul
in the summer time. Death
has a smell too, a cleaned room,

a disinfectant washed floor,
a nakedness, and a futile sadness,
for now it all begins again.
One by one they drop like ripe
fruit into the waiting basket.

There is a conspiracy of silence
behind the other doors, a frantic
dusting of ornaments and turning
out of drawers in the succeeding days.

On the day of the funeral the flowers
are returned from the hearse and they
pick them over, florist's flowers
jammed into unsuitable vases.

This is her legacy; an odour
of carnations, which masks the smell
of drains as it also masks
the fear of who goes next.

At night the lights go out
one by one as they lie alone,
waiting for the hand to shake
the branch in the invisible air.

They don't sleep well. Reaching
out to the commode they stumble
and clutch at a chair, or make
a warming cup of tea,

to pass the dawdling hours
before the dawn comes up
and they can hear the milkman
leaving a pint at the wrong door.

Silly bastard, they think, rattling
their walking frames in impotent rage,
he doesn't know she's passed away.
Nobody thought to tell him –

she is not dead but sleeping.

A Winter Affair

It was cold travelling to the coast,
standing on station platforms, rain falling,
wind banging the doors in the ticket office,
a frantic boy pacing up and down,
cracking his knuckles and talking
into the gusty air. This seemed like an omen.

October, November, December, trains
half empty, the sea like his pale blue eyes,
warmth breathing through grilles in the wall.
Brutal and gentle by turns he used her
as a groyne or a breakwater, and threw her
high into nothingness with a final wave.

Say I fed the gulls and the squirrels,
say I liked your breasts, and made you happy.
Say I am a shallow person, leching
after women, raffish and uncultured.
Running for her train she never heard
his last coarse words, his touching voice.

Mixed Infants

Mixed infants are up to their arms
in papier-mâché; a faint tapping
of rain sounds on the high windows,
and in the remedial class pencils snapping
make him think of distant canes on tender palms.

Rough justice rules in the playground,
and Carol's mum is on the game again,
to get some money for the children's shoes;
mud lies sticky as a school dinner in the lane,
and 2A sing a faltering melancholy round.

3B form pairs like old-tyme dancers,
and Darren's dad's inside for being drunk
last summer, outside the Hand & Spear,
and Sharon's brother's an exciting punk,
but no one, anymore, is lined up for the lancers.

School is out and balaclavas worn as masks
turned back to front scare girls, or do they?
Sir's wife has had her breast cut off,
they've all sung with gusto that the day
Thou gavest, Lord, is over, done the tasks

he set them. He wipes his eyes and then
locks up for the night, tells the caretaker
to wash the walls where boys who pee
the highest are admired, tries to thank his Maker,
feels a prosthesis, not a breast, and can't say Amen.

Going home, he thinks about her imperfection,
sees his mother bending to the baby,
as she once bent to him, a mucky eater,
and hears phrases like sometime and maybe,
pastes papier-mâché hope over his rejection.

Women's Surgical greets him like a man
bringing flowers to the fallen; beds
seem like tombstones. Once they were both
mixed infants, with nits in their heads,
and she admired his high arc of urine as it ran.

She is the one on the left, two beds down,
lopsided like her smile, but her kiss
is sorrow and her wound is discreetly hidden.
'Is it raining?' 'Yes, like piss,'
he says, adjusting his mask and acting the clown.

The Way We Live

Madrigals through the wall. This house
has walls as thin as tissue paper.
Sneeze, and the counter tenor falters.
Ah, Robyn, gentle Robyn, tell me how
thy leman doth, and I will wipe my nose
in time. There's no abandonment in sex.
A cry could be misconstrued as a coronary.
Look out, one parent has expired
upon the other. Anger must be muted,
vomiting, even, done with decorum and tact.
Don't retch too loud, you'll wake
the children, who will then cause
mayhem and alert the cats, who think
it's meal time, and howl in concert
at the door's crack. Life's either
a perpetual honeymoon, or suffering humanity
is at it again. Learning ways to keep quiet
in ecstasy or pain is a hard talent,
living so close. In the end,
inhibition becomes an art, like any other.
Could that patch of damp in the corner
be tears penetrating the party wall?

Blind Man in the Buff

I never thought it would be you
playing musical chairs
or blind man in the buff.

I could never see you as a guest
in the wrong house, or meeting
by chance with careful arrangements.

You were both beautiful like animals,
glossy in the pelt, doe-eyed,
so I should have known.

In fact, I could have foretold
it all with my crystal ball
and my gypsy's cunning,
if I had not been so busy
making my own illicit calls.

Welcome to the club, I could say,
but the sub is beyond our means
and the membership changes
after a few years.

It takes one to know one,
as they say in the adulterer's corner.
I have seen them clock-watching
in pubs where the seats are slit,
and on railway platforms.

They suffer. I know, because
my stretched nerves pick up
messages which are non-verbal,
tiny gestures, longing eyes.

It is all as tangible as threads
of deceit. Someone will untie
the knots and tell your wife
they saw you in Birmingham
when you said you were in Leeds.

Affairs of the heart are more like
affairs of the state. The spy
is always waiting at the gate
to intercept a message to the Embassy
of home, and send the innocent
a microfilm which should have been
destroyed and never seen.

And you cannot defect.

After Aspley Guise

Odd, how the parting made my heart
beat unevenly. Even stranger, that
familiar sick feeling and a headache
from the startling sun burning
on a pub table.
It was as if the body spelt out
the death of love
in juddering symptoms.
Someone slopped his beer
on the dusty courtyard.

Your funny lady in green trousers,
carrying her poems and scribbled notes
on how to get to Beds through Herts
watched the tin cars gathering
and the confident stockbroker-belt
people carrying their drinks
and laughing their heads off,
and saw, as in a nightmare,
the well-filled plates,
the well-fleshed bodies,
and a dog eating crisps.

The night before, Aspley Guise,
the cottage like a faded
doll's house, the early waking
to the day's planned goodbye,
the walled garden and the vine
crucified against the bricks,
late foxgloves and ferns
in the far corner.

I burn with a fever hotter
than the day's high soaring.
The Romans are marching
to St Albans. We, who were
beautiful animals, savage
each other. Baked in clay,
Dauphin. I am eaten greedily,

but now the lorries squash me
to a flattened mess of spikes
and flesh. And you?
You say I was rough –
I, who wept over dead animals.

I, who never cared for narrow lanes,
will remember a hot July day
in Aspley Guise, the cow parsley
tattering the grass verges.
I, who know the pain you feel,
notice at last the thin scattering
of birds on a refuse tip,
and know, this time
survival kits will not
arrive, or bread turn into flesh,
however paltry.

Five Finger Exercises

They were more to me than five finger exercises
as you claimed, in that first book of poems.
They were sad symphonies I could not share,
your short verses and your girls with long hair.
I never met you, and we were the wrong ages
anyway. I cut my hair off long ago,
just before childbirth. I said it was for other
reasons, but it was really the end of a way
of life which I recaptured day after day
when the letters came. You swore at me
in one, and I knew I had provoked you
into using your middle-class public school
damn. I carried the thought like a precious
parcel marked *fragile, treat with care*,
and kissed your book, and put it beside
one of my own, the sort of thing
a love-sick adolescent might do, and then

I lay awake, staring at the ceiling,
full of this unaccustomed pleasure, feeling
something had been given back to me.
Your piano keys move, and look,
no hands, no face, nothing but a letter
or two, some poems, an obstinate woman,
an impatient over-worked editor,
and five finger exercises repeated
again and again.

Stretch Marks

Lying awake in a provincial town
I think about poets. They are mostly
men, or Irish, turn out old yellow
photographs, may use four letter words,
stick pigs or marry twice, and edit
most of the books and magazines.

Most poets, who are men, and get to
the bar first at poetry readings,
don't like us fey or even feminist,
too old, too young, or too intense,
and monthlies to them are just the
times when very few need us.

Gowned like women in funereal black
they have friends who went punting
on the Cam. I'm not too clear
what others did in Oxford, except
avoid the traffic, bathe in fountains,
drunkenly, a different shade of blue.

Mostly they teach, and some must be
fathers, but they have no stretch marks
on their smooth stomachs to prove it.
At least we know our children
are our own. They can never really
tell, but poems they can be sure of.

1936

They are all massing there,
grained in black and white,
the strong Soviet faces,
turning Red Square
into a Hollywood follies,
each girl's leg a turning cog
in a precise cartwheel.
A face with the hairstyle
and moustache of my father
is held above the heads
of the marching thousands,
as the prisoners dynamite
graves in the Siberian earth,
throwing the mounting bodies in
as they arrive in even greater numbers.

You see here a delightful lady
trying on a suede boot
in a Moscow store.
It may be cold, but she is happy.
The news reel shows people
buying caviare like we buy
bread. Under the floating banners
and the tiny flags, the grand parade
goes past.
The man of steel looks out
over the heads of his
dwindling people;
purges, terrors, nightmares
flicker behind his eyes.

Treading on skulls to reach
the top of the pyramid
he does not hear the frail bones splinter,
the knock on the door beats like a drum
in his barrel chest, his outspread arms
enclose the women who were taken away
so quickly they wear the clothes
they were not allowed to change,

until the skin shows through
the worn places,
and the dead and imprisoned appear
like ghosts among the smiling faces.
The camera lies, and paranoid negatives
reveal them all, bloody banners,
like the shrouds they never had,
dragging on the ground, their footprints
white with lime, their startled faces
fixed row on row.

The Czar is dead. Long live the Czar.
Stalin once had his prison number
on his sleeve – 3316.
Profile, full-face, left and right.
It is 1936. The blood begins.
Menarche and murder link with fear
in my mind. Such a year. Such a year.

Music in a Dark Room

We listen to Debussy with the lights turned off.
The fire is warm and the day's quota of suffering
is over, and we think we are happy for the length
of a disc, for a space in time where the ear is all,
where there are no words, only notes in the fall
of the light rain mingling with his recurring
bell sounds, his embossed underground cathedral.

The old, the sick, the dying, the spina-bifida child,
the malingerer and the manic-depressive, at once
so wild, so quiet, according to the swing of the disease,
go away for this short, short time. This dark room
rings and trembles, fades, washes like limpid waves,
restores and comforts, renews and revives us,
for we need it, and so will they, in us, tomorrow.

Flying to Iowa
(for William Scammell)

I see I am your flip-side, Bill.
Now that you're into death and long
car journeys and I'm into the fourth year
of my five-year lease, it seems as if
our joke about meeting at the recording studio
was as feeble and exhausted as my body.

South to North's no problem either,
on the InterCity train to Leeds
with a dozen clapped-out faces lying
at the bottom of my bag, underneath
my pain-killers and my writing pad.

I don't notice shires, but the scenery
seems to change suddenly where great banners
of wild rhododendrons are hung along the line
to Hebden Bridge. Good Quaker country, this,
but birds, as always, I missed out on.

Your brother said we were a strangled lot,
we English. If I ever get to the States,
on this invitation I can't quite believe in,
do you think Iowa will seem outlandish?
'An English poet is a rare bird here.'
I am an endangered species, my cruel beak
poised above my soft breast, my call
repetitive and brief like an underfed child.
Will I hear mocking birds, so far north?

Man with a Plastic Heart

They cut away your heart, and gave you
a plastic one instead.
Because I love you I exaggerate.
Poets are liars very often.
It was only the valve they replaced,
but they cut your heart out, just the same.
Something has gone from you, something
has diminished you, giving you an unusual
dignity, where there was a kind of panache
before, a muscle like iron, a satirical wit,
an eye with a level and contemptuous gaze.
Directing Chekhov, your players jumped
when you chided them on, for the play
really was the thing for you.
You could have lived on your operation
for a lifetime, and yet you rarely even
mention it. You have my admiration
for this, and I do not tell you
how I see your heart like Dali's clocks
pinned outside your chest, melting slowlv
away into the landscape.
Something went wrong. They left you
with half a thumb as well, and yet
you have a heart to feel and hands
that encompass my ticking heart,
hung outside my body too,
as a friendly gesture.

Millbank

I think of the prisoners banged up
here, looking out over the Thames
from the dark side of the street.
As we climb the white steps together
and try to insert ourselves inside
one glass segment of the swing doors,
instead of two, I tread on dead faces
with my unsuitable clacking heels,
murdering the air with words.

We should have come with our eyes
held in our hands to meet the girl
holding a cat on her lap, who has,
after all, eluded us, leaving behind
an empty chair, a saucer of milk
on the floor, a note on the door.
There are cat hairs like brush strokes
all over my black jacket and bars
painted over all the windows.

We have been let out on parole
for a few hours. I have touched
her lover's statue and had my hand
cut off. You have come eye to eye
with Ezra Pound at last, and we have
picked all the erotic fruit greedily
from the cake without first concealing
a file in the middle. Outside, the wind
is as cold as an iron bracelet.

FROM **INSTEAD OF A MASS**
(1991)

Hand to Mouth

The man on the corner is selling carnations,
roses and flowers I cannot even name,
for I do not enter florists' shops,
hotel foyers or help to light the flame
which begins suburban barbecues.

The loaded barrow he owns I recognise at once,
and understand the long haul to some back street.
Later, there is a stall selling hot pies,
hamburgers and tea, but I am afraid to eat,
hand to mouth, and hurry past.

How did they trudge away slowly that year
from the piles of rotting potatoes, the smell,
the baby riding on her father's shoulders
clutching his thick hair, the one who fell
by the way, dead of road fever?

She was only eight years old, my grandmother,
and England hostile to a long-faced Celt.
When she lost her Irish name she rather
fancied her new English one, and felt
proud of her six book-learning children.

In the Lyrical Tradition

That I loved you in the best traditions
of lyrical poetry, which is where I began,
will never be remembered. Invisible
to the naked eye, the microscopic dots
form themselves into sexual fantasies.
The ear cannot hear them, nor is there
the slightest hint of salt on the tongue,
and sensations from the finger-tips
show only in the faintest trembling
of a hand on a page, writing.

Over-sensitive, touchy and thin-skinned,
I am yet the joker in the pack,
throw double sixes, climb patiently up
ladders, fall down snakes, begin again.
I prize open my diaries' brass clasps,
break a nail, a heart, rummage about
for passion, sex and art, which I
had packed away for good, and find
this lyrical poem, asking to be made,
written by a hand on a page, trembling.

Ego Trip

All you brought with you was your face,
and the keeping of a promise, two books
and that invisible companion, Super Ego,
sitting beside you in the driver's seat,
poor Libido locked like a prisoner,
or a body in the boot.

I hope never again to feel the cold
unwilling touch and the dutiful kiss.
Kind Uncle Alter Ego, who really just
came along for the ride, encouraged
you from the back seat, but cunningly
moved local landmarks.

You lost your way, confused and turning
into the wrong minor roads. No one knew
if Id was there, although he could have
been crouched in the tissue pocket,
wiping his eyes like a sad marsupial,
crying by instinct.

Too Much Angst

Too much angst, the young sculptor says,
showing me two copulating bicycles
welded in brass and the size of a hand.
Maybe, like us, they are just attached
to each other in a friendly way.
He says it's just a one-line joke,
queues up for dole money,
helps himself to coke.

I knock off sculpted icicles from gutters
in a careless way, he solders on a laughing fish,
detached and laid back as he stutters.
He plans an exhibition sometime in May.
I play around with words in the way
I do, dealing out my grimy pack of inhibitions.
He adds some floating sea-weed and a trident.
I add that touch of angst with words
he doesn't care for, brash and strident.

We don't do much good, but don't do too much harm.
He's waiting for his life to start,
I'm wondering if my fibrillating heart
means anything, but I'm laughing and he's calm.
The coupling bicycles ride off arm in arm.

You Touched Me

Never practised necrophilia
although bloody nearly
when the Major died,
four days afterwards.
Among the paras and the quads,
the neurological misfits,
the alcoholics and the shits
you were the only one
who touched me.

Touching us up
was part of the
grotesque world
of hopeless cases;
sixteen or sixty
didn't matter to them,
just the fantasy,
but you, with your
noble countenance
and your soft-spoken
innuendoes, suddenly
undid me, calling me
Sweetie like they did
in the movies.
It was crap
to get me to share
my own clapped-out longings
and worn-out flesh
but,
you touched me.

An Ideal Family

They come running through the lighted dark,
a good bunch of kids from a comfortable wife.
In the broad lap of his chair he sees them
propping him up like the cushions of his life.

As they home back, his pigeons to the loft,
he thinks of the one in the shallow grave,
the uncomfortable woman and her haggard looks
of love and her unattainable secret cave.

Celebrating, as they do so often, the ideal family
are toasting the perfection of their illusions,
and eating well in the conventional manner
he has trained them to – the master of delusions.

They come running through the darkening light,
carrying in their hands the prisoner's grain,
and the sound of their unclipped wings dies away
as he welcomes them all back home again.

Letting Go

I've always liked those grand exits;
the audience in tears, the critics
muted for once, the opera house stage
littered with final bouquets of roses.

Yet, isn't it better to just disappear,
the phone calls and letters unanswered,
letting go, and backing out quietly,
scrawling *not known at this address*.

Whoever paints the walls in this room
(and, My God, they need some colour),
should never know what went on in here,
and be grateful walls don't have ears.

Well, must close now, my father used
to write, as if locking up the shop
was a kind of rehearsal for a final appearance,
easing a muslin shroud over bacon pieces.

I've outstayed my welcome in this house,
and must pack my luggage for the journey –
some dope, some booze, a handkerchief
and a parcel of easily erased memories.

I never liked sad endings; the long walk
into the lurid sunset, FIN blotting out
the last warmth, so why do I lovingly
edit sub-titles for this silent movie?

A Straw Mat

I am guilty, she said to me. I didn't know what to say.
We are all guilty, I said, of something, if it's only living

when turf rests heavy on all the people cut off in their prime,
or buying this old cardigan from Oxfam instead of doing

something real. She said, Like what? I didn't know.
I saw my tears fall on the leper's foot. What a nonsense.

Africa is thirsty for blood and yet more blood, and we
wander round the Oxfam shop, thinking that woven mat

will do for the bit of the kitchen floor the cats leave
lion paw-prints on. *Please, I beg you, do not.* Scream.

I will and can. Blood and fear and no, no mercy
up in the top field where the bodies lie bludgeoned

and raped and still, their heads turned away, into the grass,
their legs still apart, the screams still forming on their lips.

Somewhere, someone said, 'That'll do for Oxfam', and we saunter
past the shelves of clothes, a queer smell in our nostrils,

like guilt, like spilt sperm, like reparation. We teeter
on the edge of a communal grave, clutching a straw mat and 10p.

Redemption
(i.m. H.S.)

Breathing comes as easy to me
as dreaming, fantasies come and go.
I live in another world from this.
Somewhere a man is gasping for air,
like a fish just landed on the shore.

This is another world again –
in, out, in out, in orgasmic fury,
a sour and lonely winding-in,
a gagging on terror, a taut line.

On the washed stones a thin
sprinkling of blood and the twitch
of unhooked silver bodies;
the boys scramble up the shingle,
taunting the girls behind the wall.
Hunter to prey, they single
out the one who always cries
stinking fish, waving their hands
under her nose and laughing.

Sometime just before sunrise
the nurse comes round the ward,
with her mermaid's hair tucked
under her cap, another world
from the seas she sails upon
as she sleeps through the morning.
Breathing comes as easy to me
as dreaming. I am pawning
my heart for an oxygen mask
and a silver hip-flask,
with two chances to one
of redemption.

Very Samuel

She says her cat is looking
very Samuel today.
Cats have very sideways
secret smiles, she says.
(Cats look very Samuel
when you cover their ears
with your hand.
Don't ask me why.)

Both of my cats are called
Pookiesnackenburger
for a few weeks, called
Desdemona and Othello
before that, and the vet
has them on his file
as Solomon and Salome.
(These are Biblical cats,
after a long line of
literary lads, ending with
Pushkin.)

After burying Pushkin
in a very Russian way,
with Myshkin peering
into the grave
like an idiot,
we walked away like cats,
pressing the balls
of our feet into the grass,
carrying our tails
for convenience.
(All across the Steppes
the howling echoed,
the kittens crouched
with their paws
tucked under, listening.)

Cats walk in and out
of poems, their secret worlds
as mysterious as ours.
I have just come out
of the long grass,
acting tiger.
She has seen a notice saying
GOOD HOMES WANTED
FOR KITTENS.
(Soon there will be
more cats than people,
with our hands over their
pointed lovely ears.
Don't ask me why.)

Assault and Battery

What's he in for?
Assault and battery.
Some really punchy poems
on violence, I think.

But no, the roses are pink,
there's a cottage door,
and the clouds are smaller
than a man's hand.

His paintings are bland
the art teacher says.
The cottage is there too,
and a phalanx of flowers.

Excitement grows. He is ours.
The painter and I glow
with ideas of a country
childhood somewhere.

He was reared, but where?
A slum in Hull, or Hell
or Halifax? He doesn't
quite know. Wrong again.

The shrink smiles with pain,
remembering a fragment
in the dig of therapy;
some faded floral wallpaper.

Well, we knew a taper
of truth would be significant,
and this is where his dad
duffed up his mum one day.

No, he didn't say,
but every time he'd watched
for isolated cottages
and women living alone.

Men don't bring roses home;
they plant them on women,
burn buds with ciggy ends
to keep the garden growing.

Goodnight. We're going.
He makes the screws really sick
to the stomach. They'd like
to kick his head in after classes.

Him and his bloody roses.

This Room

> *We can't really spend our whole life in this room.*
> FRANÇOISE SAGAN

Since you took me by the hand
and led me to my mother's unmade bed,
I have never got it right with men.
I remember the pale sun lighting up
the flowered wallpaper, the counterpane.

I had played doctors and nurses
in the shadowed backyard many times,
but did not think to play it with you,
although at first you were a kind doctor
and told me what I had to do.

Doing the Miserere on London Bridge
with a man who wore your thick hair
and your name and had a way with words,
I begged for forgiveness, plucking at
my nurse's badge among the crowds.

This surreal scene of secret games
is my hallmark and my contredanse,
and persuades me to bare white walls,
broken marriages and dubious friendships,
the crying voices asking me to call.

Since you took me by the hand
and led me to my mother's unmade bed,
I have waited to be shown this cell,
the healing physicians opening up wounds,
guiding me to the peephole into hell.

The Bradford Connection

(for Philip Callow)

I have been incommunicado
since I threw the gelded tree away
and looked at the unsuitable gifts –
soap on a rope, a book to look at,
a mainstream poet's collected work,
all manacled together with rhymes
and family relationships.
Christmas is when the cracks show.

I came to Bradford alone,
lying in that hotel room, curled up
in my black tights to keep
the cold away, and other things;
the TV on the wall, the old dog
playing in the yard with a ball
like an abandoned foetus,
trailing entrails everywhere.

I went to Lister Park and trod
on the long red tongue hanging
over the gallery floor. I nearly
fell on my ass, the floors were
so highly polished and Emily
under glass with her sisters,
the old books, the documents
in faded laborious copperplate.

I meant to write and say
that it's better to keep away
from my terrible dark rooms,
my artful clichés and my disrespect

for the language of flowers and hedges,
my love of gaunt and tatty cities.
My cats are like beautiful inbred girls;
they wear brown suede boots.

They sit in the lighted windows
wearing their natural make-up
and their fur coats which are
a perfect fit, watching the men go by,
the tips of their tails interlaced.
Strangely, they are as timid as I am,
their eyes shine deep red at night,
the moon silvers their fur.

A Translation

*I was a man from Japan who met you at
the poetry reading. Do you remind of it?'*

From the safe harbour of the man
with her father's name she darted
into the open sea, a small fish alive
among the sharks and smiling dolphins.
No shingle of gentility dragged
at her ankles as she arranged
the red blouse over her pregnant body
and left behind the people wailing
on the shore for medicines and love.
Only the waves queued up patiently
with white faces; passing ships
called for life-belts and bandages,
but she swam on into deeper waters,
the scarlet dye marking her progress
like a graph of feeling rising
sharply. The coastlines faintly
sketched their last pencil markings
on the horizon like a Japanese
translation of her English name,
the poem which flew to Tokyo.

Yes, Takao, I remind of it.

129

Edward Thomas at Surinders

Why am I sitting here?
I left the maps and my pipe
and my last letter to Helen
somewhere between the battle-line
and that cold new house
where the child sickened
and the joists were new.

Why didn't you bring us all?
Lorenzo would have been
at home persuading Frieda
to wear her Bavarian outfit,
but what would we have done
with Rilke tugging
at Leishman's hand?

What are these influences?
After all, you would never
follow me on those lonely walks,
your shoes highly unsuitable
and your sense of direction
ruining any compass
I might give you.

I only borrowed your voice
for a while, Edward, preferring
to play Eurydice at the pit-head.
Betteshanger is everywhere,
I find, silent in the snow.
I hew at my seam of words
in the only way I know.

Surinders: a café in West London which has poetry readings.

A Genetic Error

This is the screaming baby, arching
his back with wind, oddly dressed
in his girl's smocked nightgown,
addicted to gripe-water, rehearsed
star of their melancholy inbred world,
the negative answer to their searching.

His genes have drawn the wrong number
in the raffle of life – too many noughts
to win the prize and carry it away.
All the toyshops where they bought
his pleasures and amusements closed down
like Oxfam's riffled-through December.

This is the listening mother, writing
down his history of shrinking options,
like a character in an Ibsen play,
filling in forms for fictional adoptions,
paying her dues to foster parents
who soon tire of sick in-fighting.

There is nowhere he can safely go,
this full-grown child, except to sleep
in unmade beds in damp basement rooms,
waking suddenly at night to keep
the living wake of the walking dead,
joining the sleepers down below.

Irish Hair

Coming over from Ireland, the boat
lurching its way in snapping wind,
the decks wet and slippery with spume,
the girl, Christiana Breary,
is leaving behind the stench

of rotting potatoes, the abandoned
household goods, the shallow trench
where they left her brother
wrapped hastily in straw,
the baby dead of road fever,
seeming at the last to cry
bread or blood, and then silence.

She is nearly six years old.
When she was four it was
a fine hot summer until August
rain and biting sleet
wetted her bare feet.
She does not know that the boat
will dock at Liverpool and not Quebec,
that they will throw her mother
into the sea, free from the misty confusion
or typhus, free from the unfounded illusion
of a better life. She does not know
that she will marry into pure Norman stock,
a man gaunt as a gibbet, melancholy
as an undertaker, and that from her
will be extracted a life of labour,
but not the smell of famine or abandoning
of home and children.

They brought with them the two
brass candlesticks, wrapped
in a camisole and a pair of corsets,
the youngest riding on his shoulder.
Her father will find a new wife,
now scrubbing steps in Watling Street,
the roads the Romans made, as he
will make English roads with his pick.
She is tired of serving the gentry,
but not crying of hunger,
the basement kitchen warmed
by well-stoked ovens.

Buying my bag of potatoes I hurry
to the hairdressers. Cutting
my coarse hair the girl says:

'We call this Irish hair',
and nearly a century later I now
think of her, Christiana Breary,
my father's mother, who made
her own pilgrim's progress
to an alien land, her bible in her hand,
and in her body her unseen corn seed
which will never exorcise the devil
of hunger, or my own anger.

Imago 1943

I am aware at last that once you go
there will be no one to remember me
in just that way, or say that snow
was not whiter than my skin, which no sun
ever browned, for there is no way to know
what kind of transformation happened
to such a gawky girl, before you came.
Such short years, the chrysalis time,
and you in your cavalry greatcoat name
me wife, with my tartan cloak and green
suede shoes, and no photographs to frame,
for I was virgo intacta, in camera, imago.

From This Day On

From this day on painting is dead.
DE LA ROCHE

These radiant draped dolls
who loll in perfection before
the camera, will follow the hearse
of painting, rehearsing their faces.
Click. Click. You're dead.
They are holding the wake of art
in the Grand Salon of Paris;
the mourners are in black and white,
startled and bleached by the flash gun,
or cropped off by clumsy amateurs
as they linger by the door.

The empty house, the car parks,
the deserted street corners
are waiting for the silent murderers
to come in a blur of red,
the nudes are getting colder every minute.
Diane Arbus is recording the edges
of bleak lives and arranging
her own death somewhere behind
closed shutters on the way
to US Highway 285
with her black box in her hand.

The photographer's wife
is rarely caught in the act,
retreating from lush landscapes
and faint markings of lost villages
in colours she is not aware of.
She crosses his soaring bridges
when she comes to them, for the river
is his monochrome, and hers too.
They link steel hands rigidly
over waters deeper than they know –
not Pont du Gard, but Battersea.

Solomon's Seal

When you first gave me
the dried roots, the limp leaves,
I did not think to see
the little dangling flowers
this year, green and white,
subdued prisoners hung
for innocent crimes
under the swarthy green
of oppressive leaves.

The Requiem Mass
for dead tulips is over,
the fierce blue stars
of forget-me-nots fading
like the painted statue
I kept the first year
of our marriage, Our Lady
of the Five Wounds fighting
with the Queen's Proctor
for my immortal soul.

No confessional curtain
took me from you,
and no stitched-on yellow star
took you from me.
The clematis is doing
a crucifixion against the wall,
our vine has tender grapes.
All winter the snow
kept iron guards
in every corner.

Reading in Cambridge

I brought you here, a day
in late May, the doctor tired,
the gas and air turning the bed
into a sailing ship, nurses
into lanterns. I bled you out
to a hostile world, harsher
than the arid places
I had just travelled from,
with my faulty poems
and my Janus faces.

I left you here, a day
in early June, the poems read,
thc cycles gathered together
under NO CYCLES, New Square
enclosing the brief grass,
ignoring your timid prayer.
Addenbrooks, the brutal guardian
of the fens, raised a shout
of warning as the train
sidled through the dampening air.

I found you here, a day
in mid-July, the tablets scattered
on the floor, the sirens wailing,
the thesis papers scored
with lines, the windows pasted
over, the notice-board
empty: a near-death to call
me back with my fee clutched
in my hand, exacting your own dues,
and trailing your withered cord.

Nude Declining

Bible-backed and stiff after yoga classes
she is no Venus Anadyomene, but perhaps
was once the Venus Genetrix to her husband
and the Venus Callipyge to her lover.
Watering her maidenhair ferns alone
she remembers collapsed blancmanges
like her own heavy flesh, white puddings,
and her mother's corsets a hanging pink armour,
partnered by her father's truss, the deep bed
where a broken feather in the wing pricked
her to sleep after all those childhood sicknesses.

Meadow saffron is blooming all the year
as she washes carefully each day at those
blurred outlines, unwilling to dress herself
in dishonest clothes, defenceless and exposed
as a stony caryatid holding up a city
without men, her aching arms too thin by half.
The zinc bath no longer hangs on the door,
no corsets and trusses loop the brass bed knobs.
Turning the world upside down she sleeps
under the duvet, her leotard empty on the floor –

a nude declining.

Smile for Daddy

At last he is quiet; his harsh words
can no longer scare the living daylights
out of me. I never understood the story
they told me of him in hospital asking
to see me, dressed in my new brown coat,
aged three or four. Today I wear my black.
Bartletts as far as the eye can see pack
the crematorium pews. Don't nick the books
of Common Prayer, the gilded lettering pleads.
He would have liked to see us all walking
in the rain behind a gun-carriage, his medals
lying on the polished coffin lid,
a sort of mini state funeral, the slow drums,
the tolling bells, the black veils.

He fought, but did not bleed or die
for his country, as he disciplined
but did not love his children.
Smile for Daddy. Somewhere there's a face
grimacing at a window, a small girl held high
in the air, a pale hand waving weakly.
All the men I've loved knock on wood,
and seem to wear his humourless stare,
used me for bayonet practice, went absent
without leave, could reduce me to tears,
as he did, but they were not aware
of this, and so we wait for him to disappear,
silenced at last, although not in my dreams,
but that is my funeral, not his.

Baroque Nights and Naturalistic Days

Acquainted with baroque nights
I am not impregnated with the smell
of poverty; not my skin or my clothes.
I am a neutral and unarmed observer
making my check calls, inserting smiles
into gaping mouths and looking for signs
of leaking roofs and naturalistic happenings,
like a dead bird on the floor of a cage,
or porno-collages on dusty walls.

Acquainted with naturalistic happenings
I am dusted all over with a pollen of light
and riches of hyacinths; my skin and my clothes.
I am armed with a blade of hart's tongue,
threadbare histories rest on my time-sheet.
They have tiled over the hole where the sky
looked through, and all the baroque nights
fly away like bats in the half-light,
making murals of fantasies on bright walls.

Mr Zweigenthal

He was your other father, she said,
awkwardly. I was lucky to have
two fathers, I thought, but he was
a secret; left behind a bow-tie
like a black malevolent butterfly,
a looped violin string, an address
in Danzig, a baby in her bed.

Played beautiful he did, at the end
of the pier, the August sun dipping
slowly into the sea, the turnstile
creaking as they ran home, laughing,
sliding on shingle, clutching stones
and shells, but careful with his fiddle
and the black suit she used to mend.

What did he think, I asked, my real dad,
when he came home from India and found me
sleeping in the crib beside her?
Wasn't he pleased? Her face grew
cracked all over. The lodger, a Jew,
it wasn't meant...a mistake, the pills
didn't work. I felt so bad, so bad.

Mr Zweigenthal, I have your nose,
your hands, but no talent for a waltz,
a barcarolle. I know you almost as well
as I know myself, with your dark moods,
and your tall stooping figure which broods
over my whole life, looking out across
the Baltic, and in your buttonhole a rose.

Theatre in the Round

You were a cowardly lover, leaping dancer,
a swarthy Slav coming home after hunting,
walking more slowly as the clouds grew denser.
They roasted the pig and hung up the bunting,
but you were a yellow belly and your eyes
flickered in and out of focus, cognoscente
of failures and presidential fall-out shelters,
as they erected the swing-boats and helter-skelters.

Drifting through Soho where the clothes are scanty
and the blue movies asked you out to tea,
you never spared a caring thought for me,
crouched over the gas fire in red satin panties,
wearing my old dancing shoes, eight months gone.
Since we made our pas de deux I am all alone
except for the smallest member of the School
for Contemporary Dance, cavorting in his waters,
ready to spring naked from the wings.

I am a dressing room. I am theatre in the round.
You were my choreographer, drenched my feet
with French chalk, and my unprotected womb
with sperm, braced on your elbows, panting
into my neck. I've stuffed your letters
in the drawer with my leotards, pointing
my toes, and think of you walking in the streets
like a figure strayed into an abstract painting.

Per Fumum

Sometimes I think of your novels in the loft.
The pages are all edged with brown now;
the characters smell of dust.

I think I hear Jordan talking to Dora.
He is giving her a bottle of Californian Poppy
for her birthday, and another child.

She is pulling Patrick up Lewes High Street
on a tin tray over the new snow;
the sky is gravid over the castle.

Your typewriter is clacking in Welsh,
banging in those terrible high rooms
where the mongol children laughed.

I am combing out my hair rather slowly
and awkwardly opening my legs
to a young midwife, and we are both afraid.

We are really like people in a novel,
writing up our lives in poems and journals
and piling up cairns of words.

Inside the cairns we are playing house
with dolly's cups and dolly's pork chops
and unbreakable pink blancmange.

You wrote about a baby wrapped in a parcel
after delivery. There are babies
in the loft who won't stop crying.

I roll the agent's notes and rejection slips
into ear-plugs and think idly about
nights in the gardens of Spain.

The midwife says 'Another boy, I'm afraid'.
I roll over and reach for my notebook
and my leaky fountain pen.

One day we must clear out the loft,
and go behind the hawthorn hedge
for the ritual burning of the books.

I think the snow will be scented like Dora,
but Patrick abandoned the painted tray
for me to paint new patterns on.

Kim's Game

She ran up and down the wet streets
peering myopically into empty alleys,
fingering dhotis which looked like his,
scrabbling round the wheels of panic.
Everything looked like abandoned bazaars,
the troopers drawn out, the natives baffled
by the counter-commands of Creighton Sahib,
the quick and brutal curfew of silence.
Lutuf Ullah is gone to Kurdistan was scratched
on doors and walls. Impatient bastard,
she thought; he couldn't wait to go back
to the house with painted shutters,
the forbidden temple, the lines of words,
and the Amritsar girl turned on her side, asleep.

His disappearing act was just a return to base,
before the midnight pass ran out, and she
was only a messenger passing between the lines
with riddles for polis-Sahib, couched
in a highly emotional language, saying:
Much sorrowful delay. Rattling his sabre
he forced her to her knees and took away
her idiotic cyphers, her child's tray of toys
which she could never remember. The stallion
gallops to the North West Frontier, her father
is writing from Rawalpindi and she is not born.
She tries to think why men leave her, but all
that echoes round her mind are painted words:

Lutuf Ullah is gone to Kurdistan.

The Nuclear Girls

It has been the summer
of erotic shoulder-blades
and vulnerable necks.
Among the hobble skirts
and the ballet pumps
move the grey and black girls
with their hair on end,
as if witnessing a preview
of the burning of the world –
quiche with mushrooms.

The weather hasn't been too good
this year, but bare legs are brown,
hair has been put up
in a Madame Bonnard style,
ready for the bath.
There is something for everyone,
but nothing, it seems, for me.
I am an old man,
watching the cattle market,
eating my junk food noisily.

Decades of summers ago
I would have hoped for a glimpse
of an ankle, and never thought
there would be so much flesh
to feed my hungry eyes.
They take me to Flanders
for the day. The wars
are ghosted transparencies
of poppies and landing craft,
bully beef and hard tack.

Sitting in the sun, I think
that life has been a dream,
seen for a moment and then gone.
I would like to stroke and touch
these nuclear girls before they float
as ashes on the wind,
stripped of their crumpled skirts,
offered on the world's menu
as crêpes suzette,
or crêpes noirs.

FROM **LOOK, NO FACE**
(1991)

The Butcher-Bird

He knew about birds, as he knew about words
and the smaller bodies and insects impaled
upon twigs. He had a penchant for predators
of all kinds, and recklessly scaled
cold Everests for the ones who coarsely swore
on the summit, the winners, the flag raisers.

Climbing on to the stage, young literary fledglings
tried their wings and sang their new-found notes
indifferently. He had picked out the eggs
in the nest and already seemed to see the quotes
in pamphlets and magazines: 'this young wren
will be an eagle as the years go by.'

The butcher-bird, perched on her furthest branch
saw all the beautiful feathered friendly flock
cooing and murmuring and sharpening beaks
on bending boughs or gathering round the rock
for nesting sites. When the cock crowed
she placed her parcels on a crown of thorns.

Shifting a metrical foot, she lifted a wing
as if to salute his ornithologist's skill, found
she was chicken-hearted, after all, sorry
for her pecking ways, her shrill shrike's sound
and would have wished to be an eagle or an osprey
the kind of bird who darkens the bright day.

Of This Parish

Very ladylike, she couldn't bear a hair
unwittingly strayed upon her curling tongue.
Fastidious to an obsessional degree, she
polished her furniture to a high patina,
reflecting her anxious countenance too well.

The phone accentuated her carefully modulated
voice, but picked up a cracked and frantic note
which was not in keeping with the rest of her.
In drawers, her underwear lay neat and still,
well-ironed, aired and diligently mended.
Money was tight, and meals were very frugal,
but set nicely on a tray, cooked to a turn.
The neighbours laughed behind their hands,
not unkindly, you understand, but were not
surprised when the police and the ambulance
arrived together, one removing her correct
thin body, the other a coil of knotted rope
which they carelessly flung in the back of the car
leaving her front door locked, and picking up
a small stool which lay on its side in the hall.

Misprint

These gardens are now open to the pubic.

This duvet is all sprinkled
with trembling linen flowers;
I smooth its wrinkled
garden during open hours.

When the iron gates are shut
I open up my Venus fly-trap
just like any careless slut,
and take your head upon my lap.

You are my international trust,
selling mugs and hedgehog coasters
for the wary visitors who lust
after your maps and girlie posters.

Here are two raised white mounds
which look for all the world
like nameless ancient burial grounds,
and a smaller one with hair all curled.

These gardens are now open to the pubic
on every day of every year, the litany
gives directions in the rubric
all hung around with pimpernels and dittany.

Terrain

Hail on the wild daffodils, the hawthorn hedge
bare, the cats running, as white balls strike
their thin fur, a mad rush to the window,
and inside the smell of baking bread, the sound
of a harpsichord, a bowl of stones and shells
from all the seashores of my life.
This is my habitat.

Can you hear my feet
on rush matting as I run to meet you?
All the spiders rest easy here, the walls
need painting. There is nothing of value,
and the chairs are all uncomfortable.
I stash away your golden liquid, and water
a dying geranium cutting.

All night the branches
move against the window panes. I move
in your arms. Everything is delicate
as fallen hail, importunate as howling
cats, frail as wild flowers, hopeful
as spring in bitter winter weather.

Do not look. This is my terrain.
Why do you wish to explore it?
It is only my world you are coming to,
searching for something as elusive
as a sigh, or the sound of paws
on frozen grass, or a heart beating.

If you find it, open your closed fist
and show me the coin concealed there.
Tell me if it is heads or tails.

Pitar

'Dear Sir': he wrote to my publisher,
reprimanding him for my error
in the blurb, or so he thought!
'I am the father of the authoress,'
scanning for mistakes the copy he had bought.

All the four years in all the four seasons,
he carried his red exercise book and stub
of pencil everywhere, not asking for the reason
why he stood or lay or crouched in trenches.
No Wilfred Owen, for he was one of the men,
he recorded the weather before battles, the state
of the horses' hooves, and why there were ten
billy cans instead of twelve and grew to like
bully beef and hard tack. Reared on skimmed milk
he was homesick for his mother, and not like
his mates who missed their girls and wives.

When the eleventh hour of the eleventh day
of the eleventh month released him he became
a regular soldier with his pedantic way
of writing about all he saw and did, his stiff
sentences in copper-plate lifted from novels
as he described malaria, his temperature soaring,
the temperature outside, the natives in their hovels,
never capturing the unbelievable experiences
in that terrible and beautiful country, but wrote,
day after day, pinning down like butterflies,
the batman's name, the officers' cricket pitch.

The council flat is occupied by temporary
residents, some university pillaged his books for facts
which nobody else remembered, his contemporaries
being far too busy marrying Indian girls, or boozing
in the heat, or playing cards, not working hard
for their sergeant's stripes. He patiently wrote
his own kind of history, keeping his memsahib
tucked safely away in England with her child.
The next one to be born, spacing us by a neat

five years, my aunts all said after his funeral
that I was born cold because of his longing for the heat.

'Dear Sir, They found you dead, clutching the paper,
which happened to be the *Daily Telegraph*,
I mention this because I thought,
that, as a life-long Socialist,
this was not the paper which you bought.'

Asylum

'I am your captive and you are my cell.'
ARKADZ KULASOU

It's a comfortable cell, with a bed.
There is a Chinese blue and white bowl
for pissing in, plenty of books to read,
and nobody, mercifully, puts me on bail.

I am content to serve my life sentence,
except when I see shots of the sea,
people walking free, a complex dance
of birds in trees, just-seen mysteries.

The exercise yard is a daily walk
to the park, the corner shop, the off-licence.
Sometimes there are greetings and talk,
sometimes I huddle close to the garden fence.

I sew poems like mail bags with small stitches,
smoke my three cigarettes a day and sleep
in the afternoons and dream, which is
a freedom whose keys only I can keep.

No governor, no noisy screws, no pigs.
I am walled up here with rebellious words.
When the archeologist visits he digs
into my notebooks for labelled shards.

Letters arrive with my new number now,
flowers are left outside the locked door.
Parole is a word I don't want to know.
I don't look for your ghost any more.

The Minister's Bed

Gwyneth put us up for the nights.
the week Anna went back to Merthyr
to bury her niece. Dada was retired,
and the minister's daughter ushered us in
to the room where he and Mam had slept,
when Mam was not six foot down under clay.
Every night the eiderdown slid slowly
off the bed. We laughed and made love
under the bed clothes. Every morning
we put back the eiderdown with solemn dignity.

When the bomb came that split your head,
and split my life into separate halves,
I thought of the minister's bed,
and the way we rolled downhill naked
into the bed's deepest hollow, helpless
with choking happiness. I didn't think
to choke with swallowed tears walking
in sepia Cardigan streets, passing
Medical Hall in hallucinating grief.

I thought I saw you climb on a bus
marked Llimbo. Some Welsh place, I thought,
somewhere an enormous bed of nuptial bliss,
somewhere the smile on the mouth of a kiss,
but the driver was death, driving you off
to a narrow bed with a stone pillow.

The Wife of the Man

I have to tell you, dearest sir,
that my husband fitted Virginia Woolf
with her gas mask in 1939.
It was, he says, his only claim
to fame, that frightened face
disappearing behind a rubber snout,
like a fish drowning in air.

I would have been about fifteen
at the time and not yet aware
that I would one day marry the man
who fitted Virginia Woolf etc., etc.,
or that he would choose me
for my sick look, my thin hands,
my long brown hair.

I do not know what my father said
when he asked him for my hand,
not mentioning that he had fitted
Virginia etc., etc., but promising
to care for me, because of the likeness
to VW perhaps, my bony face,
my adolescent stare.

I have to tell you also that when
I met Leonard Woolf, taking my poems
to The Hogarth, I was tempted to tell him
that I was the wife of the man etc., etc.,
but I sank into the reeds like one
slipping into a stream of consciousness,
and I didn't dare.

Bawd Game

Do you want me brash or melancholy?
Brash, he said, for she was melancholy
most of the time.

Do you want gin and tonic or whisky?
Gin and tonic, he said, for he drank whisky
day and night.

Do you want me old or like I used to be?
Old, he said, but with the lights off,
if you don't mind.

Do you want me to shut up or hear me sing?
Shut up and have some compassion; you don't sing
very well these days.

Shall I shut the cats in the living room?
One of your cats is dying; the whole room
smells of his breath.

Do you think I should put 'he said' every time?
Not every time; it gets a bit boring every time
like you do.

Shall we play at doctors and nurses?
You know I always like doctors and nurses,
especially with you.

Would you say we look what we really are?
I'm brash and you're melancholy, and we are
fond of bawd games.

Do you mind if I have one kiss to remember?
If you smile a little, he said, and remember
to get into bed.

Join the Club

Flashing my neurotic's badge I dare them
to ask me for my licence. I don't look
much different from the rest of them –
in fact, a certain calm emanates.
I've seen and felt so much I'm like
a bird on a withered tree, singing.

Diagnosis proclaims me not psychotic.
Sensitive and shy, this patient
has symptoms of depression with a touch
of anxiety and agoraphobia.
We're not supposed to read our files,
but just the same, we do.
It's really quite interesting
the way the doctors size us up,
and there's a preening of feathers,
and comparing of notes.
Sensitive and shy sounds quite genteel,
as opposed to schizoid, paranoid
and abusive, anorexic, manic,
or simply mad.

I'm really quite presentable – not that
you could take me anywhere – I tend
to shiver and sweat in open spaces.
Still, I only suffer from a disease
as common as a cold, ubiquitous
as birds on withered trees, singing.

Poetry as therapy is not quite acceptable.
Myself, I find it more effective
than valium. It's just that if
the literary world took us too seriously
we'd be out on our necks, and ours,
like Anne Boleyn's, are extremely slender,
even if the executioner is very expert.

We are a clean and well-behaved lot,
don't need a leper's bell,

but keep our badges polished
just in case we recognise our kind.
I'm introspective. What are you?
Oh, me, comes the reply. I'm just a bird
on a withered tree, singing.

School Outing

Of course, we all remember the day they went;
Sucking lollies some were, and some were pale
And some looked distraught and miserably bent
Into cradled attitudes of fear and distrust.
The coach bounced smoothly over the unmade road,
And those at the back smiled out with wan
Important faces, one chewing on a plait, the load
Of adventure too much for the small ones,
The big ones indistinct and quarrelsome in the front.
We wondered whether it would come on to rain,
And hoped a tyre wouldn't burst or a punt
Overturn, and we saw the river run for them
And the trees lacing over their bent heads
And felt the lemonade warm and fizzy
In our own throats, and made their beds
Ready to receive them at the end of day.

What we could not have foreseen
Was that although there is always one who is lost
At the last moment, and was thought to be seen
Wandering into the bushes, they would find her,
Small Ophelia, floating near the reeds, a flower
In her hand, the one who would never know pain
Or go on a school outing ever again.

Consumers

Ask me if I ever liked
small talk, chit-chat,
the smell of a new car,
the fat freezers lingering
like over-weight virgins
in shadowy garages.
I have to say no.

Ask me if I ever liked
the long silence, full
of thoughtful emptiness,
the bruised smell
of geranium leaves,
the thin edges of poverty
like sides to middle sheets,
thin and anorexic.
I have to say yes.

Standing in Trafalgar Square
I was pleased the skinheads
ate our iron rations.
Shouting into the dark
I felt at home, the candles
in jam jars, the small group
of word-spinners,
sheltering from rain,
not ashes.

Ask me if I ever think
the nuclear winter
will be like a giant freezer
full of damaged goodies.
Lord, Lord, I have to say yes.

After the feast of flesh
and red gravy,
there will be ice cream
for afters, and then,
we shall wish we'd said no.
Lord, Lord, I tried to say no.

A Family Tradition

We should have bought pheasant
and chilled the white wine.
I don't know how to cook pheasant,
I don't know about wine.

Irish stew, eaten at the kitchen table
is not the same somehow.
There are paw marks and dints on the table.
They lower the tone somehow.

You change your shirt and socks every day,
wear street cred trainers.
I pull on my clothes reluctantly every day.
I'm too old for trainers.

It was fruit jelly you really liked,
made like your mother did.
It was your warm smile I really liked.
Do you smile like your mother did?

I never date poems; perhaps I should
to demonstrate progression.
If it would please you then maybe I should,
but there's no real progression.

My father dallied with a Professor too,
telling his war at last.
Is it a family tradition, having a Professor,
re-living old battles at the last?

Never mind the dry as dust pheasant,
never mind the wine.
You could choke to death on pheasant,
get drunk on wine.

England in January on sabbatical. Big deal,
wind and rain every day.
The poet in her natural habitat. Big deal.
Notebooks fatten day by day.

St John's Common: A Marriage

Coming down to Pevensey marshes
his white hair ruffled by the wind
off the Channel, he picked her
the purple reeds, hearing hill-dwellers
muttering, treading the pagan cemeteries
of the old Kingdom of Sussex.

He could not bring her a cinerary urn,
a fifth-century brooch, and indeed,
she scorned jewellery of any kind,
selling her wedding ring for five pounds
unaware of the over-populated seaboard
this once was, the stark Roman walls.

She was more concerned with cities,
the third world, rather than the huts
for centurions, the heavy soil between
the Ouse, where Virgie died, and Highdown
staring out across the water, the evidence
of sluices now forgotten and unused.

Coming through the hall stepping gently
on rush matting to meet him, she took
the barbaric florid purple plumes
and carefully arranged them like soldiers
holding spears, dark faces under helmets,
following the eagle, the bird of Jove.

Along the coast fossil pollen grains
and soil; and while she bound his hollow
bundle tight she filled in forms to send
to Noviomagus Reghensium, posting her FP3s
too late, signing her Norman name deftly,
dropping her coins into the Italian box.

On St John's Common where there was
very little history before Victoria, she hacked
at clay; their house rested on a raft
of concrete, the grapes ripened slowly
on the brick wall in Lewes Rape, his novels
rested too in the attic, like relics.

Coming home from Merke Dyke, he looks back
at the castle and the Norman keep, feels
the salt on his tongue, sees them stack
the low mounds of residues on Pevensey Levels.
He knows that there is nowhere she will feel
at home in her mad, sick, anywhere country.

Lamb

Scrubbing the kitchen table
after the doctor has gone,
the pink of diluted blood
and carbolic soap swirling
in the zinc bucket, her child
lying listlessly sucking a torn
membrane of worn sheeting,
dampened with tap water,
she feeds the red-eyed stove.

Now she sets the table,
sharpens the knives, spoons
fat over the lamb's leg, throws
the aftermath of surgery
down the outside drain. Her child,
sick with tears and silent
sees Abraham in a white apron;
flesh squeals and shrinks
on burning railway sleepers.

Afterwards, she clears the table,
saves the red gravy for the baby,
makes a nest on the shiny sofa,
tucking round a thin grey blanket;
her child sleeps, daubed and stained.
Steeping night-gowns in cold water
she places bread upon the altar,
covers all with a cloth, crosses herself,
darns socks over a wooden mushroom.

To Tracy with Love

He is a sensitive and perceptive man,
but not listed for the Booker Prize.
I try not to think of words like also-ran,
as he gazes for a long time into my eyes.

I hope he notices my slender wrists,
and puts me in a novel with a name
like Clarissa or Virginia, but no twists
of plot to make me older than I am.

An experience like this is lyric, brief
and limited, like a slim volume of verse
perhaps, using topics like death and grief,
a stricken woman walking behind a hearse.

I didn't tell them I am a closet poet,
and think a lot about themes like this.
I've used him in poem. He doesn't know it
yet, but I've described his first kiss.

Perhaps another poet is the thing really,
to talk about metaphors and line breaks,
but the only poet has a stutter and a belly
like a pregnant woman, and gets the shakes.

I can't help thinking it's a pity
that he gets drunk so often, when
he can't get it right and eats spaghetti
in a very sucking way like other men.

The novelist thinks I'm quite advanced
about art and literature for my age
and stroked my arms when we danced
last night, signed his name on the page.

I pack my jeans, my sonnets and his book.
To Tracy with love, he's written
in it. I wave my white hand and try to look
like Clarissa or Virginia; the nails are bitten.

Grandmother's Footsteps

Grandmothers don't wear red boots,
Tom says. Red boots and long
black skirts are what I wear,
spooning out stinking cat food,
tenderly painting brown into my hair,
swallowing vodka in the baby's orange juice
while they are not there.

The baby is being jolted along
some minor road in Provence,
and doesn't care if I wear
red boots or dye my hair.
Like his father before him,
my son is contemplating being unfaithful,
even though the baby will soon be seeing
blue shutters and vine leaves,
and his wife will start weaning
him from the breast at last,
and not a moment too soon.

Their mother is young and witty,
with her one hand clapping
and her creased blue workman's blouse
and her striped cullottes.
As she goes through the farm house
she tells Tom not to say bugger just
because I do and curses me under her breath,
shifting the baby on her hip,
poised between weaning and the next pregnancy
pouting her bee-sting lips.

I take a train to the city,
abandoning the house, the cats.
I wear my read boots and share
baby juice and vodka from my thermos flask
with you. We are an absurd and ageing pair,
flirting on the District Line,
with only enough money for the fare.

The holiday is almost over,
the baby spits out his sieved spinach
and screams his way through the nights;
I make up the cot, the beds, move a
jug of dead flowers, polish up my boots.

Clare's Poem

He was so   he was really
he was oh   he was.
He was fab   brill   nearly
seventeen   he was
really something.

Come to the disco tonight
he said   right?
Right   I said
because he was
really great right
right?

He'd got culture   he had
he went for Zappa
but he never came
He was oh he was really
a right shit.

Right?

Small Dole

I should have been warned.
You laugh too much and Latin
quips multiply like fleas
in dosshouse beds.

You are on the outside looking in.
I am the one who really saw
the dead on the floor,
laboured too long over
poems and lost causes.

I knew by your house you were not
my kind, and never could be,
although you were caring and good
in ways of the gentry,
a little patronising,
although not meaning to be.

You remind me of the ones
who worked my mother to death
and gave us clothes and smiles
and praised our hair, for theirs
was thin. Could servant's children
really have a thing called
a crowning glory?

Too late I saw I had come
up from the basement, knocked
at the wrong door, muddled
my grammar, been too much
above myself.

Brother or patron, rival or friend,
we are not the same, you and I.
Dole money is what it says.
The hungry thirties are there
for you to see in my face.

Small Dole is a Sussex place name. *Dal* has survived in Sussex
dialect speech as *dole*, used as a division of communal land.
It is a place of no importance with a few houses and one pub.

De Profundis

At the centre of the stage
she commands them to be happy.
Positive thinking she calls it,
urging them on like an evangelist.
She produces *Alice in Wonderland*
in wheelchairs, encouraging the Mad Hatter
into further madness, the dormouse
into a deeper sleep. Afterwards
she tenderly wipes bottoms, lifts them
into bed, shows them her snapshots
of Zimbabwe, kisses them goodnight.

A negative thinker all my life,
I am waiting in the wings. They cry
and swear blind they are getting worse,
pull out catheters, fall out of bed.
Suddenly, even the little speech
they had deserts them, they twitch
where they never twitched before.
Writing for me, they become miniature Ibsens,
Norwegian to their fingertips,
inhabit gloomy houses by cold seas
or learn the patter of Berryman, freak out.

I am only the writer in residence.
She re-writes their fragile histories
into brave and funny art-work, new Thurbers,
passes from one to another easily
with her curly hair and bright African clothes,
her large body and her large heart,
her everyone's mother's voice chiding.
Everyone's child, I hunch in corners
waiting for my one-line part, alert
for despair and bitter railing against fate,
altering the score from *Gloria* to *De Profundis*.

That Class of Woman

Learning that he had been called this name
by his family and friends, we talked about
Bert a bit, and then, seeing a faded
photograph of Frieda in Bavarian costume,
someone thought she looked too fat,
a stout woman who really shouldn't
have dressed like that.

Having read all the evening the work
of the man she left her husband for,
we were not surprised to see this thin man
gliding past the empty chairs –
the course was not a popular one.
By the jut of his beard we knew him,
by his welter of words, his tender care
in asking after our mothers, and he knew
us, who had left our chores and children
to come to him, reading his poems,
weighing up the meaning of a line,
watching the sun go down.

Smiling his foxy smile and smothering
a cough, he switched off the lights
and left us to stumble home alone,
and look coldly on the men we had married,
handing a child a glass of water with a remote
smile, leaving our books in an untidy pile
on tables and chairs, falling into our beds
to dream the dream of our lives, waking
to breathe the faint odour of chrysanthemums
in the morning.

Ich Könnte Nicht Gehen

What did she say? Did you hear what she said?
The shadows fall across her face like knives,
The trucks went on without her, was that it?
The faces all looked out through the slits,
Did she say? Even the children, lower down,
Their eyes showing and their hands, waving, waving.
They did not understand where they were going –
Perhaps on an outing to see the beech woods,
To pick flowers or to picnic under the trees.

Why didn't I go too? Is that what she said?
Dying, as she lived, in Hampstead, she is herded
Into the gas chambers with her family at last.
Gazing out at the mulberry tree in the garden
Her last few words were in German, almost unheard,
Lost in the frosty English air, so cold and still
Like the piled naked bodies, so soft the syllables
Melted away and the birds flew here and there,
Looking for the food she always gave them.

What could we do? We threw out the crumbs
From her last meal, and they gathered there.
For the scattered bread, flying from the branches,
Gathering in greedy groups, wings beating,
Beaks opening. Ich könnte nicht gehen,
Was it?...a train, a room, a journey.
I could not go, we think she said,
But we were never sure, as we covered her face
And tidied her crumpled bed.

Drop Me Off at the Cemetery

All the bright sun flakes shrieked up the road
leading out of town. Sitting tight on pain she told
him where to drop her off. All the Victorian angels
pointed upwards as she stumbled around mossy paths
and read the names, remembering family picnics
round her grandfather's grave, a little trowel
and the municipal watering cans, unaware of loss,
heeling in the plants her grandmother handed her,
imagining the roots creeping down to fill up his eyes
and his mouth, and the hand which used to cuff her ear.

Other hands, which had plucked lightly at her, as if
afraid to touch, held the wheel firmly as he turned
on the motorway, heading for home, could never
have fashioned the wooden spires her grandfather made,
but chiselled neat lettering on her very bones,
handed her an inbuilt watering can, eye-shaped,
to water the flowers which bloomed in early spring
and summer with names like love-lies-bleeding,
or forget-me-not, bedding plants with just a short
time to live and a concealed poison in the stems.

Cemeteries are very comforting places; levelled off,
laid low at all ages, there's no way of telling
who loved who, she thought, and who would have liked
to dance on graves or jumped in with the corpse,
a provincial suttee; dragged out by relations,
muddied, blotched and ridiculous, carted home
back to an empty house, empty glasses, ash trays,
and a tape machine which picked up the wrong voice,
clicked, wound on, stopped, recorded, played back
with a relentless and pursuing theme of factual data.

Again

He is teaching *Middlemarch*. Again.
I come from Des Moines. Somebody had to.
How is the weather then? Tell me.

She is doing solitary stubbornly. Again.
Send me letters from the Mid West.
I need to see you smile, your sunlight.

We are looking after the children. Lovingly.
That is what holds us together,
the little watching faces, the baby dinners.

How can you say I don't love you?
You are dreaming about Kristen. Again.
Your hand is only six inches away from her.

Bernard is writing to Cynthia. What, again?
Your friends are always so weird.
I know. None of them are quite sane.

Jim Agustin is holed up in Manila Metro.
Yes, again. *Miss Saigon* is playing here.
I don't go to London now. Too much pain.

I could teach *Middlemarch* on my head.
Who is sleeping with who on campus?
I think I'm falling in love. Again.

Clusters

Natural skinheads, learning
about the sickness therapy,
they ride the ward's rocking-horse
on good days, go home sometimes
to the one concrete tumour
which never shrinks,
attached firmly to the spinal
curve of a northern coastline
and the abandoned foreshore.

Diamonds for the rich demand
this word, shafts in mines,
pillars, columns, piers –
all are clustered.
Groups of persons, animals
baby-fine curls
on infant brows in
the nineteenth-century novels I read
for my balding tutor.
Also floribunda roses in catalogues.

Herself Alone

The day Declan died we pulled the blinds,
huddled in the parlour, drinking whiskey,
singing the old songs, stoned out of our minds,
propping himself up between the sideboard
and the piano, cursing like hell, the black flag
tightly jammed in the sash window, the rain
coursing down the back alley. The kids
were out early waiting for the telly men
to come, thin boys hiding the stones
in their pockets and little else to do
until school should start again. Herself alone
sits in the kitchen, sober as a judge,
fondling her rosary, not seeing, not hearing,
not weeping, and entirely out of her mind.
Three boys and not one of them alive now.
Three boys, and the pulling down of blinds.

TWO WOMEN DANCING
(1995)

A Nodal Point

I wasted my life on this:
it was friend, family, lover.
When rejection came it was
on a slip of white paper.
Acceptance arrived similarly,
signed Ed, promised a fee,
brightened the day unexpectedly.

My heart was held tight
in a clamp, a vice; my anger
burned with a fierce white light;
all my life was exposed on paper,
and never lived, except haltingly.
Now, at the nodal point, I see
urgent buds on a dying tree.

I have come so far to find
the shadow of my father's hand
making rabbit's ears on the blind
for a frightened child, and
see him looking kindly upon me.
That I once loved unreservedly
is now clear, at last, to me.

from **Going Home***

1

Goodbye Nowshera. A soldier's Farewell!!!

Pindi, Lahore, Agra, Old Delhi,
the city walls pock-marked
by cannon balls, the Mutiny –
some part of history he was not
called on to enter, the sun
drying up the blood too soon,
his wife and child living their lives
in rural Kent, waiting for letters
with bleached and faded stamps.
On the train a tea-planter is taking
his mad friend to England.

2

I and my corporal tenanted empty padded cells
on my tour of duty. We found them not too bad.

He saw the tea-planter's friend weeping
on the deck, babbling on about a kite
drowned off Bombay, thrashing about
in the filthy waters, becoming part
of the garbage and excrement he foraged among.
After a few hours in Aden the ship passed
through Bab el Mandeb. Africa rose sheer as
Dover cliffs as they steamed up the Red Sea.
The Rev. Mr Broughton read from his Bible
about casting out demons.

* Extracts from my father's journal, *c.* 1924.

After Aden he thought about the baby,
now a frowning four year old.
The next one, he was sure, would be a boy
and named after him. How his wife cried
the night before he went to embark,
her broderie-anglaise nightgown wet
with tears and milk, her long brown hair
over his face, in his mouth, his eyes.
Brown as the Indus.

My wife did not know me, for she had not yet
recovered from the effect of the anaesthetic.

When they pulled the big girl from me
I did not know who I was or why this soldier
stood at the foot of the bed. Mother,
I said, and later she told me about the ether.
I was sick all over the counterpane. Mother,
I said, and then he went away. I thought
I would lose my mind with grief, but this
was not the way of it all.
He will come back.

We berthed against the quay wall at Port Said.
I noted a distinct change in the weather.

It was as hot as hell in Aden, although
hell is really cold, all hung about
with blinds and ghosts walking the decks.
The young soldier writes in his diary,
and my friend tastes tea all night
in his sleep, talking to himself.
India, India, my country, my wife,
where shall I find you again?
His mind seems calmer, like someone near to death,
after malaria; the wind blows from the North.
The young soldier shows me photographs –
a handsome woman holding a child,
like the statue in the Cantonment church.
The Rev. Mr Broughton has his face
set towards England and does not hear
our prayers. He does not ask what kind
of visions my poor friend sees.

3

I had no further use for my drill clothing
and dumped it overboard with my sun helmet.

As the ship passed the great green statue,
a body was seen floating for a while.
Coaling was over, the Victorian bedroom
appeared like a vision, the rosebuds trailing
over the walls, his wife putting her arms
round him, the child asleep in the next room.
The Rev. Mr Broughton says a prayer for the dead,
but it was only a bundle of drill clothing
thrown overboard by the young soldier.
This he will always remember.
She will always remember the long nights
in her mother's house without him.

So we went below, bidding farewell to both Asia
and Africa. Well on the way now!

My mother smooths the sheets and reads his letters
for the last time. She dreams they throw him
into the sea. I think he sails in a paper boat
to come to me. He will bring me the sun
in his kit-bag, the sun and the moon and the stars.
I will say to my friends that I have a father too.
My mother irons her best nightgown and then
she washes her hair and puts me to bed
in a small empty room for the first time.
In the morning my muslin dress hangs
on the door where the ghost moved last night.
I am a big girl now and I can show you India
on the map. It is coloured pink.

Embarkation Leave

It was Egypt where the rot set in,
after all those anguished meetings
and partings; then embarkation leave.
His blond hair was almost white
as he slouched around the markets,
stumbling by accident it seemed
into the red light district, the boys
who sucked him dry, the thin girls
with babies left behind in villages
along the Nile, who taught him how.

After a second stroke, the brain scan
shows the seeping liquid as a shadow.
He is always packing up his kit,
ready to board the ship of fools,
and she is waving him away, wearing
her tea-rose honeymoon underwear;
Southampton broods darkly just behind
the early morning light. But now
she washes through his rubber pants
and hangs out his sheet like flags.

This is the worst time, before he loses
sight of England and doesn't know
her anymore as she hauls him out
of the bath like a flying fish, the sea
flooding the tiled floor inland.
In the officers mess he feels the heat,
the stained armpits of his uniform
an army's changing maps. Picking up
his topee he heads for Cairo and the bars.

Antosha

What are the streets of Taganrog like these days?
If you look very carefully, you may see a thin man
with a beard and pince-nez glasses and a little cough
leading the child he once was as they pass through
the shadows to the local store. It is between lights
and the past and the present are interchangeable.
He did not live at any time at all, because
he will always live.

If you were walking in the Black Forest when the train
went through to Moscow, with a wagon marked OYSTERS
in the heat of a summer day, were you aware of a coffin
inside it as it went slowly past, the bright sun on the rails?
Were you even aware that it was 1904 and the month was July?

Sometimes, over the sea of Azov seagulls swoop and wheel
in mewing plaintive whorls. Notice carefully if one dies,
or there is a handkerchief stained with blood on the shore.
You might find one anywhere in the world, if you search
long enough, but you must smile and pick it up,
but do not call a doctor, for there is no need.
He is already there, and if you too are sick,
he will come to you, but he will not ask you
for a fee.

Recantation

A sliver of limelight, some free booze,
a box of books, a cold river smell
from the Thames. The sounds they made
were not the sounds lying quietly
between the covers. They double-crossed
their art, wore their faces out smiling,
topped up the glasses and scratched each
other's backs. The words wept in the pages
for their masters, who recanted, laughing.

177

Tundra

The empty page is like the tundra,
where any mark might show from a plane
in an aerial photograph, where herds
of animals seem like moving question marks,
the weakest ones the dot at the base
of the curve, travelling slowly.

To travel slowly is never to arrive
at new feeding grounds, to lie
a heap of bones, picked bare –
no head-stones for caribou or moose –
just mild hat-stands littering ihe ground,
the sub-soil frozen solidly beneath.

There is a tundra of the mind,
bleak days of hungry endurance,
a blind movement onwards, an instinct
to go forward with the rest,
whatever the cost, only to join
the few who inhabit the dot.

The few who inhabit the dot, lie
listlessly, like-minded beasts,
chipped hooves moving feebly,
eyes rolling like marbles,
giving up the ghost with breath
like untended whistling kettles.

West Pier, Brighton

This is a frantic place,
full of the sea surging,
boats drawn up on the shingle,
smell of tar, frayed nets,
salt-clean stones, pier supports rusting,
Victorian machines half-working,
jerking heads from the guillotine
into doll-sized baskets.

Madame, the sea is slowly crawling over the esplanade,
seeping through the streets and washing out
the lettered sticks of rock from the beach huts
on the littered foreshore.
Shall I have my photograph taken in the musty booth?
The result is a ravaged slattern with tow hair
blown back from a wrinkled and sweating forehead,
waiting for execution, trundled through the streets
to die on a rotting pier
in bad summer weather.

Albertine, I beg you, hurry the children along;
the fires are burning on the beaches, the young
are lying in the shadows, navel to navel,
their eyes half-open, so many we shall tread
on them as they lie like seals basking
in the darkening light.

Give me back my head, and re-assemble
the grotesque scene in the machine.
Did I come here to be cut down?
Whitebait is being served in the grand hotels,
hamburger in the sleazy back streets.
I have no taste for anything.
Let us go back to where we came from,
whoever's children we took there,
whichever century it was.

Madame, allez vite; it is coming on to rain,
scribbling away at the sea with random pencil markings.
We shall dream as we die, and the curving waves
will cover us all.
Who will follow the loaded tumbrils?
It is over. We are sleeping,
the pier is dying slowly,
the machines are out of order.

I tell you, Albertine,
the whole world is out of order.

The Puffin Mortality Rate

The puffin mortality rate is high.
People tread through the snow with
a Parkinson's soft shoe shuffle,
recovering on pavements cleared
like corridors of hope. No Russian
hats anywhere. Children are taking
giant steps for mankind in red
and yellow moonboots. Say cheese,
we say, say Dangermouse, say thank you
to the old man of America.

Our fat tabby cat swallows her hormones.
She is living out her ordinary cat life
in this extraordinary house, thanking
the drug company for her paunch
and her life. She sits among the toys
with her eye-liner on and her way
of sounding like an urgent phone call.
Say who likes frozen Bird's Eye puffins,
we say, say Bagpuss, say knock, knock,
who's there? Nuke Lear.

Back down. It's summer time. Wave goodbye
to the kind men who left your eyes out.
Who are all these cyclops children
blindly groping along our northern walls?
We're wearing bikinis now, or nothing
at all. Sorry you were spawned here.
Baby, it's cold outside. Goodmorning,
Britain. Say three blind mice, we say,
say I saw him die with my little eye,
but there's no one to hear.

Egg Tempera

He will not eat, for his cause
is freedom. His jailor is four
times his size and yet she is crying.
The hot prison shows him bibbed
and with a jaw which she cannot
prize open, for force feeding is jibbed
at. He is two years old.

In their happier moods she calls him
her little love, her no no bird,
lowers him on to his lonely pallette.
He will surely dwindle away into
nothing, her stick-like martyr,
diapered hunger-striker, play-dabbling
in egg tempera.

By now they know the score, as she
cooks his dinner, puts it in the bowl
and watches as he tips it on the floor.
All the little shells of pasta
lie like abandoned pallid molluscs
on the water-colour patterned shore.
How long can he go on?

No doctor ever saw a young child
die of hunger in the middle classes,
finger-painting gravy frescoes
on the wall. A mild icon haloes
his defiance, like an H Block inmate,
and the garbage can is overflowing
with cold scrapings of independence.

Sanctus

Put out the light, lock the door, play the sanctus again
And again, and again. Something must be salvaged,
Something must be saved.

Forgive me. I must go back
From where I came, before we found the paper bracts
Of mallow blooming in the narrow lane to Morwenstow,
Before the high shoulder of the cliff leaned over us
At Tresaith, before we crossed the sea to Caldey Island,
Before the rocks and the boulder and the sea-thrift.

The moon gives a bright enough light for one
In a double bed. I will take care of the cats,
And you will shrug into your parka, roll up your maps
And go, and we will meet, as parents do, in Cambridge
For graduation day. I shall wear my cloak,
And you, the only good suit you have left.

What flowers bloom in that flat Fen country?
Marsh marigolds and lady's smock, and sometimes water
Forget-me-nots. On the downs above Lewes the cowslips
Are out, and in lonely places, the rare orchid too.
Up on Ashdown Forest tall companies of foxgloves
Gather to assault the enemy of memory.

Forgive me. The mass is over. The flower has withered.
You have drunk my blood, and eaten my unwilling flesh,
For the last time.

Life-Style

Maculinea arion,
the Large Blue butterfly has gone:
next cowslips, or even us.

The flower heads of wild thyme
hold the pearly eggs. The habitat
is all wrong, its life-style
too complicated, like ours,
all wrong for today.
The ant mistakes it
for its own larvae
when it falls to the ground.

Large Blue, you're tricky
and mean, eating up the grubs
you resemble, growing fat
like a cannibal chief.

If the Adonis Blue goes too,
there will be two less blue
butterflies left to settle
for a moment as you lay
after a wild time of loving,
eyelashes making butterfly kisses.

The ant is stroking the caterpillar
like I stroke you. In the Kafka
corridors of the ant hill it grows
large and pale, paying its keepers,
sleeps, eats, and finally spins
a pad of silk the length
of a menstrual cycle,
until it finds its own way out.

Wings still limp and small,
it hangs on bending grass, dries,
and suddenly flies
up and away for ever.

Below the Cotswold hills the cars
queue up for petrol, steel-blue
and far away as ants. On back seats
your father's butterfly book,
full of outdated information,
reports strange histories
of finished mysteries.

Blue Buildings in Hove

Once I gave a talk on García Lorca, years after his death, and someone in
the audience asked me: 'In your "Oda a Federico García Lorca" why do
you say that they paint hospitals blue for him?'
from PABLO NERUDA'S *MEMOIRS*

Wandering in dark streets there were
no taxis in Barcelona; just empty shops
and cafés serving lentils, tracer bullets
making patterns in the sky, the maps
spread out like well-worn love letters.
You write to say that the tourist peel
has been carved off with a scalpel,
revealing the orange, Spain, beneath.

I go to see Paul in Hove. He is sharp
as a knife still, peeling our poems
like decadent fruit. Julian says
I am too young to remember and indeed,
I can only just see the hostile dark
Basque children behind the trestle tables
at school, and you going off to fight,
the letters from the fighting arriving,
cracking jokes as brittle as dead bones.

Among the poets, you patched them up,
for, newly-qualified, you left Cambridge
and Barts behind with your practical jokes,
your medic's rags. You still do clinics
in Hove, twice a week, to keep your hand in.

All around are blue buildings like liberty
and joy, and your Communist banners
rot in the garage. I send you greetings.
Surgery begins at five in the afternoon.

Midsummer Common

From white bird featherless, the snow
begins to look like discarded detergent,
blows like powder, and is no longer welcome.
On Midsummer Common children avoid it,
this thin scattering, too small to build
a solid man with eyes of stolen coal.

Straight from Siberia, across the fens,
the wind brings cries through frosty air
from half a century ago. If only we knew
the Russian alphabet, or could hear the words.
Cambridge's joke becomes a multitude of voices,
calling through the splintering wastes.

Too cold to be sad, we walk warily across
the pristine paths to school, your hand
in mine, your easy tears frozen on your face,
and no more to come, for you accept the gates
of iron and the playground's brutal noise,
the red summer kites discarded on the floor.

From your fever's candle which lit up
the icon on the wall, this first day back
seems like a prison sentence for a crime
you cannot understand, the six-pointed stars
scratched on the window and the cat, Myshkin,
left upon your bed licking his fur boots.

Everyone is drawing snow, painting snow,
writing about snow. Someone is sick in class.
You were surprised it wasn't white, and came home
handless, came away friendless, came back landless,
wearing your shoes on the wrong feet, as if
you should go barefoot to the college wall.

Art Class

There is much that should be altered here.
The cloud in the left-hand corner
is not really necessary.
The two people who stand by the door
of the farm look far too homely.
I would transfer them to the fields,
with bent and aching backs,
hoeing turnips, but not picking strawberries,
I think. Strawberries smack of decadence,
bringing marquees, or debutantes,
or even fêtes to mind.
The tree which stands behind the house
is too stark, so why not make it two.
And remove the birds.
Yes, cut out the ornithology.
People see too much of them anyway;
two wings, a beak, legs like an undercarriage.
Give me your brush,
and I will paint them out, so that it will be
as if they never dotted your canvas.
The light's not bad, not bad at all,
but it isn't the kind of light we like to see
in paintings nowadays. Rather sombre,
I thought, as if the two lonely figures
in the field might soon pack up
and go home for tea.
This is the trouble with your work, you see:
it seems to have a life of its own.
For myself, I would have them drinking wine,
and lift the whole lot from Wales to Brittany.

Love Poems

He made poems like very weak
academic tea, all the correct
classical allusions, but all
the incorrect ways of slicing
meat very thinly to save money
eluded him. Instead his work
was like pink tinned ham,
although he'd seen all the right
paintings in all the right
Art Galleries, and knew
his Bach from his Melba.

A nice fellow (a real Fellow –
not feller, as in yeller,
or in man), he trod the party line
at May balls, and never
mentioned the other kind,
but bit delicately into his
strawberries, sipped his wine,
dined in Hall sometimes,
and wrote his lines
with a fountain pen.
Biros were not for him.

Only his friends knew
his love poems were
for other men, and that
he could be seen at dusk
outside public toilets,
appearing to be studying
the writing on the wall,
or reading his book
on a park bench when
school was over for the day,
waiting to be asked to play.

Blurb

She read English at the local public library,
got a B.F. for fouling up the assembly line,
did a postgraduate thesis on the influence
of early poverty and the care of siblings
from the middle classes. It was not accepted,
although she shortened the title afterwards
to *The Meaning of Weaning*, and later took up
Sociology, not the first to use that new
well-known seat of learning, The University of Life.
Her papers on the care of terminal cases,
the future of the feline race and painting
by numbers were widely acclaimed – well,
in some places, except by those who knew
she watched people too intently and called
moussaka a kind of foreign and outlandish stew.
They saw through her closed confessional curtain
and listened to the paltry faltering tales of sin,
knew her as a bastard child, hesitant and uncertain.

Tigger Ward

When he came to Tigger Ward,
he knew he was dying,
but had to pretend in case
he made the nurses unhappy,
so he fashioned a brave face
out of the plasticine they gave him,
and put it on each morning
although his hands appeared
to be touching his face and ears.

Sometimes the ones from Wol Ward
came to play, but, lying
playmates that they were
they pinched his arms
and clicked their Rubik cubes,
and went away, leaving
a disturbing smell of recovery
and a pile of comics,
the sinister Mister Men.

He knew that when Eeyore Ward
got hold of him, crying
would be allowed at last
but he remained dry-eyed
knowing she would be there,
all day, all night, kidding him
on about summer holidays
and jolly little journeys
to the carping silly sea.

Passing through Pooh Ward
on a trolley, the sighing wheels
sorrowful beneath him,
he arrived at Piglet,
the treatment room,
but before they could string
his feeble trotters to the rail
he was up and away, floating
over Five Hundred Acre Wood.

They donated a bed in Tigger Ward,
as if they were buying
him some kind of immortality,
and wrote him letters
in the local paper.
'Dear Kit, We all love you so.
Happy to the last.
Missed by all his little friends,
and Mum, Dad, Nanna and Gramps.'

Entering Language

Mothers remember the first word,
rising like a stone in a stream
of babbling. I hear the word *dot*
from my miniature pointillist
unsteady in his painted cot.
The first snow, and *Dots, dots, dots*
he cries with the eloquence and tone
of a lay preacher spreading the word
to a deaf world. We are as ecstatic
and amazed as Seurat discovering
the phenomena of vision. In his world
of wooden bars and hemispheres
of milky white, dots surround us
for a few days, stars are pin-heads
at night, sugar glacial specks;
we dot and carry one, hear Morse code
in our sleep, wake on the dot of six.
There's no doubt we are all dotty,
but soon we are into language,
no pause each day for breath;
linked words, sentences gather momentum.
Dots all gone away, he greets the sun.
We welcome him into our world; he picks
out commas, colons and full-stops
to please us, but Os are more exciting.
Oh, we cry to everything, but it palls
at last; the Great Os of Advent
turn into yawns. At dawn we hear him
trying out the seven antiphons and groan.

All My Daughters
(for Nicki Jackowska)

When we were all drunk, and you
were clutching the black man's arm
and laughing like a child under the trees,
I thought I should have ironed your blouse.
Poor girl, Ma would have said, to wear
a crumpled rag like that, never understanding
the casual stance of a young poet
up and coming, wearing a school beret
without a badge, last year's leather boots,
her sister's skirt nearly to her ankles.

When we had all celebrated the four triangles
and the boy from the burning bush,
it was no good trying to put out the blaze
with a half of lager and a lecture on money.
It would have been better to use the beer
to damp down the blouse and have done with it.
Leading us through the jungle of streets
and ha-ha among the strumpets, we came
hot-foot to the underground city, leaving
the bearded chieftain to slip away unseen.

When we settled for the journey back
and you mocked my burning of the books
in the pedestrian precincts all laced around
with new, new supermarket wrappers
I thought I should have fed you with more
than an apple. There's enough going round
about an apple and a tree and a serpent, anyway.
Ma would have given you a good hot meal
and a decent blouse and rubbed up your spectacles
so that you could see the world clearly again.

When I got off and, waving all down the line,
carried my disease under my hat so carefully,
back to the little house where apples lay
in solid rows like decent Socialist parents
I counted out my pain like loose change

from the pockets of my life and studied
my five-year lease to make sure it was all
in order and will you my copy of Karl Marx,
Ma's diabetic diet sheet and the love
I send now after chemotherapy and orange juice.

X-Ray

Here we see the delicate white curve of the hip,
bone meeting bone in such fragile-seeming structure,
arch and span of a human body, all flesh stripped
and dissolved in the bland dark, under the red eye,
in a moment of fear and lost dignity.

Already the machine has achieved
what the grave will do more slowly.
Already upon the mounted earth lie grieved
messages, tied to withering flowers among
the scattered dead. In this room
we see only the bright architectural square,
and the pale distribution of miniature tombs,
the dermoid cyst with its teeth and hair,
held in a shadowy void between hip and breast.

This is a life. She sees the hands
of the young Jew, and feels the cold embrace
of the cassette, and all that life has been so far
is the damp leaves in the school grounds,
and old magazines in endless doctors' waiting rooms,
Sir Lancelot among the reeds, and the sweet sounds
of a badly played flute one summer evening
in Lowndes Square.

We may perceive the endless succession
of barren years, but she will always
be waiting for the flute to sound again,
and the promise to be fulfilled.

Minder

This is a voice I could
fall in love with.
Even *use your goddam head*
and *get the hell outa here*
sound like a caress
or an invitation.

Corn country. He pilots me
through the readings,
gets students off my back,
sees how tired I get,
and how suddenly,
sells my books,
buys me ice-cream,
travel sickness pills.

I'm afraid of the flight back.
He's crossed the pond
so many times he thinks
I'm fooling around.
Don't get many stiffs,
except from boredom.
I settle like a child
with a Seidlitz powder,
sleep, wake, arrive
at last to grey rain,
flattened musty hay,
the mammary downs.
Your folks gonna meet ya?
I'm going home alone,
but he doesn't know this.

At the ticket barrier
English flows like tap water.
Thank you so much,
most kind.

The readings are over.
I feel as if a great

peering yellow sunflower
has been torn up
by the roots.
Write me. I shall.

Sheep country. I dream
of flying. Chicago,
Minneapolis, Iowa…
I am coming I am coming.
The headless lambs
hang on hooks
in your chilling rooms.

You are the boy
who leads me to
the sacrificial stones.
Sure thing.

Letter from Australia

This is the best hand I can manage.
It is like writing in handcuffs.
I cannot walk very far now.
This is a diabolical disease.

A flight of white cockatoos at Whittlesea,
over the new house; kangaroos, you write,
grazing in the paddock. Do you remember
the roo you accidentally hit coming home
from a holiday? The children wept,
the blood flooded the windscreen,
the whiplash injuries have all been kept
as mementos, written up again and again
in case-notes, medical mysteries,
neurological histories, childhood traumas,
graded in lists of intractable pain.

A sculptured wall of snow here in Kent,
forged by the wind in the Isle of Grain,

seagulls flying inland. I write in bed,
after watering your African violets,
and try out poems in my head, turn over
images of accidental deaths or the fight
for breath. Fast as leaping kangaroos
or quick as cockatoos in flight,
I know what I would choose for you –
a hire-car kamikaze – driving like hell
along the road to Manuka late at night.

Silk Cut
(for Fleur Adcock)

We have been sent out
into the garden; a pink
paper lantern moons
uncertainly above the lawn:
we may smoke out here.
Inside the room, the guests
sit round the table,
talking and not smoking;
a baby appears to be floating
in a green glass bottle
high on the basement wall.

Cigarettes in mauve and white
packets ease our consciences,
and possibly our lungs.
We are sensible people,
when we are not smoking,
or writing, or falling in love,
and we have met again
for the third time,
as social pariahs.
The smoke curls up
into the late summer evening
like small early bonfires;
the flowers do not cough

or turn away. We have
drunk a modest glass or two
of wine and flicked our ash
onto the mown grass:
we do not speak of nicotine,
but children, cats, and books.

Stubbing our cigarettes out
onto a white saucer
we turn back into the room,
cleansed, purified by fire,
ready for the late jokes
about sexual disasters,
the laughter, and the black coffee,
which we refuse.
You feed the cat cold turkey
under the table, looking out
at the unremarkable garden;
leaves like black silk cutouts
shiver against the mauve sky
streaked with white
and a hint of red.

Tender Loving Care

This nurse is far too involved with patients.
A short spell in Casualty should remedy this.

Her voice was too strong
for him, the glottal stops
blunting her sharp tongue
and the anger frightening him.

He had buried his young
mother after the freeze frame
of paralysis, the movement gone
where such beauty had been.

He never said what they did
with the horse. If it died

too, nobody mourned it, and if
it lived, nobody loved it either.

She was too late with cards
or flowers for a tall fair boy
with the tic of trauma hovering
round his eyes to this day.

How tenderly she felt
he never knew, for she had
built a wall higher than the one
which once surrounded them.

Lost early to her own parents,
she was like the soft flesh
of the limpet, clinging to rocks,
hidden inside a shell of loneliness.

That he looked for mothers
in his women gave him a kind
and gentle way with them
and they held up their babies

for his admiration. That she
looked for fathers in her men
was more disastrous than death
itself, paralysing her love,

and sending her to the beds
where only the mute and imprisoned
heard her changed voice, felt
her soft hands stroking them.

Half Holiday

So I loved you then, and traced your name
Upon the dim outward window of my room
Enfolded in the splendid tortuous gloom
Of most utter loneliness, before you came.

I sought you often when you knew not
And on swift sun-pierced half holidays
The wooden floors of public art galleries
And the red plush seats of too hot
Concert halls became my searching places.
Sorrowfully, you stared from the plaster cast
Of the white-faced Schumann; the last
Great cries of symphonies and the sweet spaces
Of slow movements became you, and in the shadows
Of dusty boxes you moved, you gripped the rough
Curtains and pressed your face into the stuff,
Hiding from the programmes' fluttering snows.
Sitting in the tram, bodies jolted, swayed
Towards me, touched and departed, leaned
And were gone, leaving the imprint of your limbs
Upon me; spasmodic shivers of light and shade,
Hands suffused with knowledge of the world,
The bent coiled head like a tulip bloom
Broken near the flower, the wavering boom
Of the mid-way traffic – all lay curled
Closer to me, made heavy with meaning in you.
The cloaks of Polish officers swung
On the stairs after the ballet, swayed and swung
In folds of remotest and most curving blue;
Their strange voices sliced up the moonlight
Till the segments writhed and quivered and struck
Upwards to the blank shop windows
And you returned to me through their night.

So I found you in the spitting men, at last,
And the pregnant women;
Crouched in the pages of Flaubert and the plaster cast
Of the white-faced Schumann:
I fumbled then, most bitterly with words
And sought you in most utter loneliness,
But the days returned your image;
The galleries gave back their promise.

Working the Oracle

Upside-down kitchen table,
relegated fur coat and red river
meet on Friday mornings.
They are like three sisters,
deploying agoraphobia, depression
and epilepsy on cardboard discs
for his eyes alone.

Upside-down kitchen table
moved into the shadows, she says,
the first day at her Catholic school,
trapped by the door, abandoned
by her mother, wishing herself dead,
but unable to live or die,
locked in a sulky limbo.

Fur coat in the wardrobe
feared her father's hand, raised
when she least expected it,
saw her grandfather's globular head
like a ziggy light bulb, pre-empting
fits and starts and auras,
forecasts of prismatic tears.

Red river, seeping gently,
stopped several times on the way
to a calculated calvary,
splashed blood on book covers,
school desks, taut draw-sheets.
She gives birth to herself.
He is the midwife.

Cathy, Angie and Lizzie
play Furies, Graces, Harpies and Nymphs,
fight with the world, the flesh
and the devil or Tripitaka,
form Pythagoras' perfect number,
arrange the triple thread
into coherent mythologies.

The shrink floats them
down the river to Delphi,
cuts red umbilical cords
like ribbons from the navel
of the earth.

Roman Carnival

The Count's mistress feeds the hungry cats
of Rome. Her hair is like coiled eels,
and her novels are selling well these days.

She has quite forgotten her English lover
and the gawky girl who sleeps at night
with cats humping the duvet beside her.

The novelist's lover has only a pet rabbit
and is no longer young, his one eye staring
at death and despair and the waiting gulls.

The gawky girl has been given a kitten
and called it after a character from Cranford,
having tired of Proust and The Bible.

The kitten is lying on her back, exposing
her shaven side and the one neat stitch
which means she can never become a mother.

The man, who has met the young girl at last,
fancies a Siamese cat. He had one once before
when he lived with his wife in Rodmell.

The Communist's mistress has a cat who eats
rabbits and envies the young girl her poems.
She never goes to Moscow, nor, indeed, to Rome.

She too has almost forgotten her lover,
and also the gawky girl; the eager novelist
reads Cranford sometimes, or The Bible.

The arrogant cats everywhere yawn and wash
and sit on the proofs of novels and poems
and manifestos, practising their predator's ways.

After the carnival they come out of the shadows,
carrying away scraps of food and lives,
scattering to underground galleries and holes.

The gawky girl feeds her hungry cats at home.
Her hair is half-way down her back, and her words
are flying over the page like frightened birds.

Two Women Dancing

Q. What are two women dancing?
A. Bread and bread.

There was the bread
sinking into buttery milk,
slowly expanding islands
in a white sea,
my mother's oil slicks
glistening a false gold.

There was the bread
my father delivered daily,
those whey-faced babies
lying on slats of wood,
warm from the oven,
tissue-paper shawled.

There was the bread
we cast on the waters
for ducks and swans
on the skin-flush green
of the canal, the empty
bag like a collapsed lung.

There was the bread
dissolving on a tongue
which had not said
the words of attrition
or learnt the language
of funeral clichés.

There was the bread
clasping pale slices of ham
like pink bookmarks
on journeys to prisons,
the train eating miles,
a greedy child.

There was the bread,
finally, pushed through the bars,
a useless fare, spat back
in words I'd never heard,
two women dancing,
bread and bread

Appointment

Tell me about yourself, he said, and she
was astouded to be asked, watching his tea
cooling, as she explained about her dreams
and how she spent her nights in sordid scenes,
cleaning out her own particular Augean stables,
or frantically placing food on empty tables.

Why do you think this is? he said, and she
cleverly side-stepped the trap of mythology,
explaining about not being able to cope with
children, husband, love, and that other myth
of women who could sew and garden, bake
and remember the sequence of pills to take.

Well, let's see, he said, watching her as she
wept, the tears rolling down like a rosary,

sliding down her face and neck, her white
blouse stained with milk, her hands quite
still in her lap, and he fingered his pen,
wishing she'd stop, and wondering when.

I'll see you again tomorrow, he said, and she
got out her handkerchief and mopped feebly,
blinking through the prisms of her private world
at his solid form, his neatly parted, curled
white hair, knowing it was useless to say,
I won't be alive when tomorrow is today.

Gods

These gods. Who are they?
There's Mars. I know him.
He likes mushroom pie
rising in the sky.

The God I feared
disappeared
a long time ago,
and the young man
with the blond beard –
pure undiluted
Aryan stock –
has a pain
in his arm, holding up
that light
for so long.

There was Tess,
who would dangle
beautifully, her damp dress
flapping round her legs
when the gods
had finished their sport
with her.

Some Greek god or other
is kneeling, etched on a tile,
bought at the airport
to while away the time
until the next flight.
The courier takes fright
at tales of wax
on the runway,
but the weather is fine
and no feathers float
from the sky,
the sun is just far enough
away.

Ye Gods and little fishes.
My English mistress
is exploding to the class
of '39, about to pass
on the dubious message
that the word is God.

Marriages

The bride wore white; her stomach bulged a little.
She rested the Victorian nosegay on her three month
foetus. The groom wore black, his mouth was dry,
and in his morning suit appeared to be in mourning
for his life, as Chekhov said, but in a vastly
different context.

The ushers whispered sibilantly *His or hers?*
The red bricks of the church, like sliced offal,
formed a back-drop for the tense precarious
ceremony. The bridesmaid wet her knickers.
It was nerves and the very cold weather
which did it.

Bored, the congregation waited for the words
and vows and hymns to end, shifting

numb arses on the wooden pews, thinking
of the booze-up to follow and the buffet
prepared by the bride's mother, who showed
the strain.

The vicar sucked his antacid tablets noisily
and wondered why he'd hurried his lunch
for this poor lot, standing and sitting in all
the wrong places, tense with hostility,
eager to be gone, having done the right thing
in the wrong way.

Somewhere, real marriages are consummated
without signatures and rituals and pealing bells.
Outside the laws of church and state they take turns
to cook the supper, live happily in sin, open
like flowers one to the other, see visions,
hoard treasures like misers.

The Key to the Garden

There was a London square. There was a garden.
There were people in brightly coloured clothes,
moving here and there among the trees. Sandals
touched the sunlit grass, bare arms were raised
wine bottles uncorked, glasses, held up to the sun,
sparkled and glowed. Trash cans filled up soon
with cardboard plates, mouths were gently wiped
with crumpled paper tissues; the dead flesh
and the fermented grape clustered round
back teeth. Somewhere flowers were crushed
in idle hands, bushes were flattened against the railings.
The trees stood around like guests, waiting to be
asked to join in, filtering the slanting rays
as they fell on gleaming heads and moving hands.
One lifted up a root and inched forward slightly.
The happy people were so drunk by now
they didn't notice the trees getting closer,

and wandered into the little sunlight
there was left, and lay down together, talking
softly and nibbling each other's ears.

The trees began to interlace their branches,
it grew dark and then darker still.
They thought the bands of twined leaves
looked decorative around all the white throats,
until the communal scream stopped echoing
round the stuccoed houses and the garden
swiftly resumed its natural shape again.
The garlanded bodies of the beautiful people
as they lay among the wine bottles came from
the elegant rooms they would never see again.
The men who came to cut down the trees
carried the gilded corpses away as well.
Real estate is booming. All the tenants
have a key to the garden and the saplings
are daily growing faster.

Rocking the Boat

You were right about rocking the boat,
and I do take care since they caulked
me up and painted me black and blue
for the Spring. I report any leaks
and check out the places where limpets
might grow and fill my sails taut
in the wind as I round the headlands.
I always know when it's best to make
for harbour and tie up for a while.
The harbour-master beds me roughly
between canvas sheets with his cruel
smile and his rigged-up ardour.

I am high as a kite in the punishing gales,
shouting into the wind and adjusting
the sails without any crew, except for

the ship's cat and you. She doesn't like
to get her fur wet and craps in the galley.
You were right about rocking the boat.
I do take care, but the quick-sands suck
harder than a hungry baby. It's just
bad luck that the mariner's graveyard
claimed me, that strong winds blew me
and nobody knew me, as I hit the last flare
and threw it into the whimpering air.

Accidental Death

I write to tell you that the fairground closed
after the deaths of all those children flung off
the roller coaster like a screaming white foam
interlaced with red. After all, enough is enough,
everyone seemed to be saying with their mouths
stretched into ovals of amazement and horror,
until the thin lips of funeral faces borrowed
for the day shut tight under eyes set back
in their heads like burnt holes in a limp sack.

I write to tell you this because a fairground
becomes the most desolate place in the world
when the generator stops its energetic hum
and everyone goes home before the lights unfurl
on their improbable tawdry blossoming trees.
This is how innocence ends, and all the seas
are halted to collect the dead from shores
of trodden grass and diesel oil, and where
the last cries of terror hang upon the air.

I write to tell you that the fairground is a dream
which is never interpreted by any bawdy shrink.
It opens up each night for those of us who pay
the price of being left behind, willing to drink
the fizzy lemonade of fantasies, or suck
the ice cream of oral delights, forever stuck

in the turnstiles with the wrong kind of money,
pleading innocence and turning deaf ears
to the carousel's terrible aftermath of tears.

Colour Code

I was blue to start with,
herding my patients
into the interrogation chamber,
taking down names and numbers,
but week after week
I looked upon the indigo people
with that touch of envy,
determined one day to join them
if I could.

Sometimes I feel very orange,
fading quickly to yellow
at literary parties,
bumming my way round
Universities and Art Centres,
green and passionate
in hotel rooms afterwards,
thumbing through the colour code,
fingering my cheque.

I shall never be black
for these are rare and dangerous.
Nevertheless I talk to one
in extremis. No church
holds him and he has no creed.
He is often silent,
circles higher than space,
has not yet given me the signal
to go.

If I become an indigo person
(sensitive, intuitive?)

I shall eye the violet people
with the same kind
of feverish longing and desire.
Somewhere once I was red,
drinking straight vodkas in pubs,
my sharp elbows angled
like weapons.

Meanwhile, I flick through
the colours until the spectrum
dissolves into purest white
(like a pale moon?
like a blank page?).
When I lose my gender
and my name
I shall be nothing,
no colour at all.

Wouldn't She Just

Force-fed, held down by nurses, some ate
with her. Catatonics, mute for a decade,
talked to her; yet she was mad herself.
Wouldn't she just, yes, wouldn't she just
avoid the bang of the locked ward door.

One of the privileged, she issued books
from the hospital library for those
who still wanted to read, wheeling
the trolley with infinite love and care,
kept her long hair shining and neat.

She had done well, the committee agreed,
and, no longer under order, was allowed
home, carrying concealed in her bag
the tablets she had hoarded, laid
down and died, fell asleep reading.

Friendly expanses, horrid empty spaces, *
she had studied her Balint diligently;
a model patient she had co-operated well,
but in the end decided it was no go,
fell soundlessly through friendly spaces.

* Michael Balint: 'Friendly Expanses – Horrid Empty Spaces',
International Journal of Psycho-Analysis (1955).

The Group

The leader is a caring person.
He demonstrates this with his hand
on my knee like a dead starfish.

The group is very understanding
when Cassie has a lengthy dialogue
with her dead mother and starts to cry.

The joker tries to make us laugh,
but we don't laugh too loudly
in case we offend someone's psyche.

We are all ears, inclining delicately,
full of true feeling, and (could it be?)
compassion. Yes, we think so.

A weekend of soul-searching, two days
of learning to cope with stress.
My God, I think I'm finding it all

too stressful. We stand in a circle
with our arms round each other,
breathing deeply in and out, and sweating.

The last night we edge away nervously.
The leader looks quite lost, sitting
in the circle of empty chairs.

After the role-playing we go home
to groups who never listen to a word
we say and don't even meet us at the station.

Case Notes

1. *Antenatal problems*

I have been taken over by an invader
with a changing face and gills,
whose final chords I dread secretly,
but who brings gifts and smiles.
Each morning I sicken, but the violinist
I slept with practised his scales on me;
his tune is as desolate as a dirge,
his wife is the theme of his concerto.

2. *Infant feeding problems*

This mouth turns away from my sore breast
and then screams like a soprano in an opera.
I walk the lonely rooms night after night,
thinking I might pick up a pillow as a mute,
and listen to the quiet largos again.
Murderous and tender, I begin to think
of sterile bottles in a fridge, a xylophone
with correct hammers to strike the right note.

3. *Maternal anxiety*

Sometimes I am tempted to walk away, leaving
the conductor with his baton raised,
an empty chair in the fifth row, one less
oboe player who throws the whole symphony
out. Timpani beats in my aching head,
and in dreams I lay down my instrument
in a warm bed, shawled in white voices,
glittering coldly in the early dawn.

4. Family planning advice

They offer me pills or coils or celibacy.
The bass player has fathered four; he thinks
his children will all be musical like him.
On Sundays they all jump into the car,
and he flies kites, mends broken dolls,
catches the plane at Heathrow, fathers
another after a world tour. I fumble
with devices with trembling clumsy hands.

5. Bereavement follow-up

It will all pass. All passes, someone said.
The foster mother says it shocked her badly,
and the coroner records a cot death.
I was rehearsing so I am not to blame,
but all the same I am half a bar behind,
swallow crotchets whole, listen to words
like lyrics for an unknown composition
in a language I have not yet learnt.

6. Suicidal adults

The last great chords fade away, chairs
scrape, we troop out into the snowy streets.
Snow could cover and kill; just one night
of exposure. Night is a cacophony of cries
arpeggios of tears. I strangle in clefs,
draw semi-breves tight round my throat.
I ring the violinist and he says it is all
for the best. I scratch finis on the door.

7. Necropsy report

I am filed here, edged in black as if
I had died a century ago. I am the one
described as the body of a young woman,
slightly under-weight, with normal functions,
and extremely long fingers, suffering from
post-partum depression, for whom a stomach pump
was too late, and who could easily follow
a complicated score, but had no encore.

Themes for Women

There is love to begin with, early love,
painful and unskilled, late love for matrons
who eye the beautiful buttocks and thick hair
of young men who do not even notice them.

Parturition, it figures, comes after, cataclysmic
at first, then dissolving into endless care
and rules and baths and orthodontic treatment,
Speech days, Open days, shut days, exams.

There are landscapes and inscapes too, sometimes tracts
of unknown counties, most often the one great hill
in low cloud, the waterfall, the empty sands, the few
snowdrops at the back door, the small birds flying.

Politics crop up at election time and ecology
any old time, no ocelot coats, no South African
oranges, a knowledge of the Serengeti
greater than the positioning of rubbish dumps
here in this off-shore island in hard times.

Seasons never go out of fashion, never will,
the coming of spring, the dying fall
of autumn into winter, fine brash summers,
the red sun going down like a beach ball
into the sea. These do not escape the eyes
of women whose bodies obey the tides
and the cheese-paring sterile moon.

As you might expect, death hangs around a lot.
First ageing mothers, senile fathers; providing
the ham and sherry when the show is over,
examining stretched breasts to catch the process
of decay in time. In farmhouse kitchens they make
pigeon pies, weeping unexpectedly over
curved breasts among the floating feathers.
The men tread mud in after docking lambs' tails,
and smell of blood.

Chronology of poems

1941: 'Design'.
1943: 'Half Holiday'; 'Southover'.
1944: 'Loving Neighbour'; 'Tresaith'.
1945: 'School Outing'.
1949: 'Deviant'; 'The Minister's Bed'.
1950: 'David in Roma'; 'Multiple Fractures'; 'Schizophrenia'.
1951: 'Degrees'; 'Ian, Dead of Polio'.
1952: 'Neurosis'; 'The Child Is Charlotte'.
1953: 'Lisson Grove'.
1954: 'A Pastoral Crime'; 'Heart and Soul'; 'Second Wife'.
1956: 'Autumn Evening in the Provinces'; 'Baroque Nights and Naturalistic Days'; 'Birth'; 'Old Movies'.
1958: 'End of a Marriage'.
1959: 'There Is a Desert Here'; 'The Way We Live'; 'Waiting Room'.
1960: 'Disposing of Ashes'; 'That Class of Women'.
1961: 'Front Parlour'.
1963: 'I Am That E'.
1964: 'Guitars as Women'.
1965: 'Therefore My Grandmother in Sepia'.
1966: 'Betteshanger'; 'Consumers'; 'Psycho-Geriatric'; 'Quite a Day'; 'Rumours of Wars'; 'Saint-Severin'.
1967: '999 Call'.
1968: 'Mr Zweigenthal'; 'Music in a Dark Room'; 'Polling Station'.
1969: 'An Answer to Blake'; 'W.E.A. Course'; 'Yesterday's Face'.
1970: 'Cold Turkey'; 'Night Duty'; 'Opting Out'.
1971: 'Per Fumum'.
1972: 'Troller Fratrum'.
1974: 'Man with a Plastic Heart'; 'Theatre in the Round'.
1975: 'A Winter Affair'; 'Contre Jour'; 'Farewell Gibson Square'; 'Goodbye Dan Defoe'; 'Immunisation Day'; 'No Rain on Campus'; 'The Old Workhouse'.
1976: 'Corpus Christi'; 'In Memory of Steve Biko'; 'Lyke Wake'; 'My Five Gentlemen'; 'Not Dead But Sleeping'; 'Painting of a Bedroom with Cats'; 'Red Cell Precursors'; 'Safe'; 'The Intruder'.
1977: 'Five Finger Exercises'; 'Mouths'; 'The Visitors'; 'Tripos'; 'Unrequited Love'.
1978: 'God Is Dead – Nietzsche'; 'Man Eating Apples'; 'Surgery'; 'Will the Real William Morris Stand Up?'.

1979: 'A Wrong Kind of Levitation'; 'Voyeur'; 'X-Ray'.

1980: 'After Aspley Guise'; 'An Ideal Family'; 'Charlotte, Her Book'; 'Drop Me Off at the Cemetery'; 'Edward Thomas at Surinders'; 'Mixed Infants'; 'Strange Territory'.

1981: 'A Straw Mat'; 'Front Door'; 'Government Health Warning'; 'Ich Könnte Nicht Gehen'; 'Inner City Areas'; 'Irish Hair'; 'Letter from Australia'; 'Mistaken Identity'; 'Sasha's Room'; 'The Butcher-Bird'; 'To His Dry Mistress'.

1982: 'Look, No Face'; 'Mademoiselle Miss'; 'With My Body'; 'You Touched Me'.

1983: 'A Good Old Bed'; 'A Perilous Zone'; 'A Translation'; 'Blind Man in the Buff'; 'Gods'; 'Hand to Mouth'; 'Imago 1943'; 'Life Style'; 'Misprint'; 'Sanctus'; 'Student Demo'.

1984: 'A Plea For Mercy'; 'Blue Buildings in Hove'; 'Blurb'; 'From This Day On'; 'Pitar'; 'The Bradford Connection; 'This Room'.

1985: 'A Genetic Error'; 'Assault and Battery'; 'Asylum'; Chapter Headings'; 'De Profundis'; 'Ego Trip'; 'Flying to Iowa'; 'Kim's Game'; '1936'; 'Of This Parish'; 'Reading in Cambridge'; 'Salad Dreams'; 'Solomon's Seal'; 'The Wife of the Man'; 'Tigger Ward'; 'Very Samuel'.

1986: 'Art Class'; 'Bawd Game'; 'Egg Tempera'; 'Love Poems'; 'In the Lyrical Tradition'; 'Join the Club'; 'Letting Go'; 'Millbank'; 'Recantation'; 'Silk Cut'; 'Smile for Daddy'; 'Terrain'; 'Too Much Angst'.

1987: 'Midsummer Common'; 'Minder'; 'Nude Declining'; 'Redemption'; 'The Puffin Mortality Rate'; 'To Tracy with Love'; 'Two Women Dancing'.

1988: 'Grandmother's Footsteps'; 'Lamb'.

1989: 'A Family Tradition'; 'Again'; 'Antosha'; 'Clusters'; 'Herself Alone'; 'Marriages'; 'Some Misunderstandings and Other Things'; 'St John's Common: A Marriage'.

1990: 'All My Daughters'; 'Embarkation Leave'; 'Entering Language'; 'Roman Carnival'; 'Themes for Women'; 'West Pier Brighton'; 'Working the Oracle'.

1991: 'Tender Loving Care'.

1992: 'Wouldn't She Just'.

1993: 'A Nodal Point'; 'Appointment'; 'Case Notes'; 'Colour Code'; 'Rocking the Boat';

1994: 'Accidental Death'; 'Going Home'; 'The Group'; 'The Key to the Garden'; 'Tundra'.

Index of titles and first lines

(Titles are in italics, first lines in roman type)

www.ingramcontent.com/pod-product-compliance
Lightning Source LLC
Jackson TN
JSHW020019141224
75386JS00025B/590